Between Sundays is a wonderful resource for Christians who understand that life in Christ is lived every day, all day long. Our worship on the Lord's Day and our collective Bible Study with our brothers and sisters in Christ are integral to our relationship with Christ and His body. However, our everyday lives in the world are also evidence of His presence in our lives. They provide opportunities for us to be salt, light, and leaven in a world that is often surrounded by darkness and doubt. Steve has done a great job of reminding and encouraging us to live our lives fully, joyfully, and completely committed to Christ "Between Sundays."

Sheila Butt
Former Tennessee State Representative
"Sisters, Servants, Soldiers" Ministry

Christianity isn't finished at the end of Sunday worship. Steve Miller's lesson book, *Between Sundays*, identifies the necessities of daily Christian living. The emphasis is on biblical expectations being expressed as specific personal resolutions—a good study for both private or class use.

David R. Pharr

BETWEEN SUNDAYS

STEVE MILLER

© 2019 by Steve Miller

All rights reserved. No part of this publication may be reproduced, stored in a retrieval system, or transmitted in any form or by any means without the prior written permission of the author. The only exception is brief quotations in printed reviews.

ISBN-10: 1941972934
ISBN-13: 978-1941972939

Published by Start2Finish
Fort Worth, Texas 76244
start2finish.org

Printed in the United States of America

Unless otherwise noted, all Scripture quotations are from The Holy Bible, English Standard Version®, copyright © 2001 by Crossway Bibles, a publishing ministry of Good News Publishers. Used by permission. All rights reserved.

Cover Design: Josh Feit, Evangela.com

CONTENTS

Introduction	7
I Will Observe the Lord's Day	12
I Will Live By Faith	20
I Will Hide the Word in My Heart	29
I Will Love with Heart, Soul, Mind, & Strength	39
I Will Be Salt, Light, & Leaven	49
I Will Serve	59
I Will Practice the Golden Rule	68
I Will Walk Using a Moral Compass	78
I Will Work Honestly	88
I Will Balance My Responsibilities	101
I Will Pray Without Ceasing	111
I Will Fulfill My Role in the Home	120
I Will Be a Faithful Member of the Body	131

INTRODUCTION

Christianity is a lifestyle. It is a worldview. It is a way of life. Disciples of the Master Teacher, Jesus Christ, live and function in a world that is largely opposed to the Savior and His followers. Conversion has changed our status from being in the world to now being "in Christ" (Ephesians 1:7; Galatians 3:27). By continuing to live in the world, we have an obligation to worship God faithfully each Sunday, the first day of the week. We are also called to live a daily life of submission and obedience to Christ in all things.

ORIGINAL INTENT

The early Christians' example of dedication to observe the Lord's Day each week and daily live by faith, despite persecution, was due to having walked in the footsteps of the One who died for them. In other words, they lived the Christian life between Sundays.

> And they devoted themselves to the apostles' teaching and the fellowship, to the breaking of bread and the prayers. And awe came upon every soul, and many wonders and signs were being done through the apostles. And all who believed were together and had all things in common. And they were selling their possessions and belongings and distributing the proceeds to all, as any had need. And day by day,

attending the temple together and breaking bread in their homes, they received their food with glad and generous hearts, praising God and having favor with all the people. And the Lord added to their number day by day those who were being saved.

Acts 2:42-47

Should we not be as close, unified and dedicated as the early church? Do you remember your conversion to Christ? This is the pivotal point in one's life; making the decision to make Christ our Lord and Master. Post conversion finds that the concept of ownership has changed. It is no longer "my will" but "His Will." Christ's sacrifice purchased us from the slavery of sin and freed us from captivity to make us servants of righteousness (Romans 6:15-19).

To many, the concept of "church" is the building. The term "sanctuaryism" denotes the idea of a sacred place. Application is made today by relating our Christian faith to what takes place inside the building on Sunday. However, the church is the people, not the building or meeting place.

What has caused this misunderstanding?

1. Membership mentality: Now that I am a member, I can show up now and then and everything is all right. My name is in The Book of Life (Revelation 21:27), I am secure; now I can relax and take it easy.

2. The Sunday morning only syndrome: In some places, a significant portion of the attendance Sunday morning is that of individuals who are not fully committed to Christ and His Church. Have we been guilty of patronizing this crowd only to allow them to feel secure in their relationship with God?

3. The tendency to compartmentalize our "church life" and our "daily life" (work, family, school, social, community involvement). We deceive ourselves into thinking Sunday fulfills our obligation for the other six days.

The truth is, God demands our complete attention, devotion, our ALL! C. S. Lewis illustrated this when he wrote:

> Christ says, Give me All. I don't want so much of your time and so much of your money and so much of your work: I want You. I have not come to torment your natural self, but to kill it. No half-measures are any good. I don't want to cut off a branch here and a branch there, I want to have the whole tree down. I don't want to drill the tooth, or crown it, or stop it, but to have it out. Hand over the whole natural self, all the desires which you think innocent as well as the ones you think wicked – the whole outfit. I will give you a new self instead. In fact, I will give you Myself: my own will shall become yours.[1]

Let us give God our whole being every moment of every day of the week.

CHAPTER SYNOPSIS

> Therefore, my beloved, as you have always obeyed, so now, not only as in my presence but much more in my absence, work out your own salvation with fear and trembling, for it is God who works in you, both to will and to work for his good pleasure. Do all things without grumbling or disputing, that you may be blameless and innocent, children of God without blemish in the midst of a crooked and twisted generation, among whom you shine as lights in the world, holding fast to the word of life, so that in the day of Christ I may be proud that I did not run in vain or labor in vain.
>
> Philippians 2:12-16

---

1. C.S. Lewis, *Mere Christianity* (New York: Touchstone Book, 1996), 169.

Paul encouraged the saints at Philippi to persevere in living the Christian life every day by working "out your own salvation with fear and trembling." Christianity is to be lived out between Sundays. Chapter one presents the importance of the Lord's Day in Christianity. Sunday has fallen upon hard times in our current culture and we are reminded in its observance how God desires it be utilized.

Chapter two highlights our living daily by faith which is practiced in obedience to God and results in good works.

Chapter three serves to remind us to continually study the Bible. Tragically, God's Word is being neglected, and we should be like the Bereans who examined the Scriptures daily.

Chapter four develops the teaching of the two great commandments requiring us to love God with our heart, soul, mind and strength, and also love our neighbor as our self.

Chapter five uncovers the Christian's duty between Sundays to be salt, light and leaven, which refers to our daily example.

Chapter six examines how the Christian is a slave of Christ and in turn a servant to all.

Chapter seven explores the words of Christ when He said: "So whatever you wish that others would do to you, do also to them, for this is the Law and the Prophets" (Matthew 7:12).

Chapter eight calls us to live holy lives and be aware of the dangers of the lust of the flesh, the lust of the eyes, and the pride of life.

Chapter nine reviews the role of labor in man's existence and looks at the Christian's position in the workplace and touches upon five of the challenges we face in our culture.

Chapter ten is an appeal for the servants of God to be balanced in the activities of their daily lives. Busyness is sometimes viewed as being productive and this false view is exposed.

Chapter eleven relays the importance of prayer by examining the attributes of God and how the more we know Him, the more beneficial our prayer life will be.

Chapter twelve in *Between Sundays* discusses God's plan and role for the home in society. We need to know and fulfill our individual roles. The chapter further examines marriage as God ordained and originated it is the only authorized arrangement.

Chapter thirteen provides a Scriptural prospectus for the Christian as a member of the body of Christ, the church for which Jesus died, and highlights some challenges and solutions that permeate the church today.

The chapters in *Between Sundays* remind us of the lifestyle that follows Christ in every way, all the time. Christians do not take vacations from their faith. Being a Christian is who we are *Between Sundays*.

1

I WILL OBSERVE THE LORD'S DAY

Sunday, the Lord's Day, has fallen on hard times. What was once a day of worship, family time, sharing meals, visiting with neighbors and friends, has now evolved into secular activities and work-related duties more than ever before. Does the Lord have a day anymore? John MacArthur has observed how historically Sunday was a day filled with spiritual activities and devotion to God:

> But it was supposed to be a day when everything sort of came to a grinding halt, and we set it aside for contemplation of the Lord, reading of Scripture, reading of Bible stories, reading of Christian books or theology, talking about the things of the Lord, and most importantly bracketing the day in the morning and the evening with the worship at the church, and throw in Sunday School and maybe youth group before Sunday night, and it filled up the day.[1]

A changing culture, and the fact that we live in a post-Christian America, reminds us that we no longer have the privilege of Sunday being structured like that of a century ago. We face reality while longing for simpler, more meaningful times. The tidal wave of

---

1. https://www.gty.org/resources/sermons/90-380/Why-Sunday-Is-the-Lords-Day.

secularism has affected the Lord's Day. "Services are shorter, more superficial, and fewer, at a time when they ought to be deeper, longer, and more frequent." [2]

We need to slow down, and declutter our schedules, especially on the Lord's Day. Will our focus be turned once again back to God, family, food, rest, devotion and neighborliness, on Sundays?

The apostle John said, "I was in the Spirit on the Lord's day" (Revelation 1:10). The day belongs to the Lord. Are we in the spirit as well?

BIBLICAL IMPORTANCE OF THE LORD'S DAY

The importance of the Lord's Day is verified by the great events which happened on that day in history.

1. God created light on the first day of the week (Genesis 1:3-5).
2. Jesus was resurrected from the dead on the first day of the week (Luke 23:50-24:3).
3. The Lord's church began on the first day of the week (Acts 2:1-47).
4. It is the day the Lord's Supper is observed (Matthew 26:26).
5. It is the day we give financially to support the Lord's work (1 Corinthians 16:1,2).
6. It is a day of worship and singing (Hebrews 2:12).
7. It is a day of preaching and teaching from God's word (Acts 15:35).

WORSHIP ASSEMBLY

Worship is something a person does. By its very nature, it must

---

2. Ibid.

involve an expression or action. One cannot worship God acceptably without the proper attitude.

Worship is to be offered to God faithfully. Worship must be intentional in order to be pleasing to God. God is pleased when our worship is accurate and authentic.

We congregate, or assemble (1 Corinthians 11:17), to worship God. The New Testament only authorizes five items or avenues through which we worship as a congregation of the Lord's people on the Lord's Day:

- We Celebrate: Sing (Ephesians 5:19);
- We Commemorate: Lord's Supper (1 Corinthians 11);
- We Communicate: Teach/Preach (Acts 20:7);
- We Call upon God through Prayer (Colossians 4:2);
- We Contribute (1Corinthians 16:2).

Worship is participatory. We must be participants, not spectators! We are not the audience; God is. Many come to be entertained. This is why we hear "I don't get anything out of the worship service." True worshipers are a part of the service and actually come to put something into it. True worship is a giving experience.

THE DEMISE OF SUNDAY FOR GOD

Reggie Joiner, in his book, *Zombies, Football and the Gospel*, has a chapter titled, "Sundays Are For Football." Another writer stated: "It's time. Time for pro-football fans to once again worship at modern-day cathedrals known as stadiums. Time to gather in homage to that autumnal sporting rite—the first Sunday of the NFL season."[3] The movie, Concussion; based on the true story of the doctor who discovered CTE, (chronic traumatic encephalopathy) in football players is the story of a major battle the doctor faced with the NFL

---

3. www.usatoday.com/travel/.../2003-09-30-football_x.htm.

in bringing the information to the public. The movie shares the lead character being told he is "going to war with a corporation that has 20 million people on a weekly basis craving their product. The same way they crave food. The NFL owns a day of the week. The same day the church used to own, now it's theirs. They're very big."[4]

What does that tell us? "Americans may not know who their god is, but you can be sure most know who their team is."[5] We are enamored with extra-curricular activities. We should certainly not circumvent sports and the arts in our lives, recognizing the value and benefit of such activities. Recreation is necessary to help balance our lives. But the questions surface, are we filling our time with activities to the neglect of time with God?

What about the Lord's Day? An all too familiar scene is of members leaving as soon as the Lord's Supper is completed to head to the 'event of the day,' whether it be football, baseball, basketball, hockey, tennis, concerts, dance recitals and any plethora of other things.

Other members miss the worship entirely. Many do not return on Sunday evening because they are tired from the day's activities, or the event is still in progress. There are parents who miss worship to attend these activities, setting an example for their children stating God does not come first. In an article titled, "The New American Religion: The Rise of Sports and the Decline of the Church," Albert Mohler describes the situation by observing:

> In a real sense, big-time sports represent America's new civic religion, and football is its central sacrament…The massive rise of sports within the culture is a sign and symptom of the secularization of the larger society…Secularization does not necessarily mean the disappearance of religious faith, but merely the demotion of religious involvement and identifi-

---

4. https://www.nationalreview.com/2016/01/concussion-will-smith-confronts-diversity/.

5. http://www.albertmohler.com/2014/02/04/the-new-american-religion-the-rise-of-sports-and-the-decline-of-the-church.

cation to a level lower than those granted to sports.[6]

Where does the Lord Jesus fit into our passion? Church and worship have become an event; IF it fits my plans for the weekend.

Sports fans in general are known for their loyalty, dedication, and deep commitment toward the players involved and the teams they represent. In many cases, fans will go to extreme lengths to follow or support their favorite player or team.

There are certain characteristics of fans that should mirror our dedication to Christ and His Church. For example: They arrive early. They are not concerned with how long the game or match utilizes. Overtime is welcomed. The dedicated sports fan will endure any kind of weather from freezing temperatures, snow, sleet, rain to the burning heat and humidity. The best possible seats are sought after, preferably close to the action. Many never miss a game. The sports fanatic can memorize statistics and know the standings list by heart. Money for tickets is not a problem because they are more than happy to pay the price. You will not find a more vocal proponent for their favored team or player.

Now apply these characteristics to our Christian service and worship. Are we more committed to our favorite sport, hobby, movie star, musician or other individual than we are to Jesus Christ? Do we show up early to fellowship with our brothers and sisters and to welcome visitors? Do we engage in worship without being concerned about the clock? Is it easy to forsake the assembly when less desirable weather conditions prevail? Are the seats in the back or near the exit more appealing? Are we faithful to be at every service (Hebrews 10:25)? Do we know the Word (2 Timothy 3:15)? Do we have portions and passages committed to memory (Psalm 119:11)? What do we sacrifice for God (Romans 12:1)? Christ? Church? Those in need? Are we willing to spend for the Lord and His work (2 Corinthians 8:5)? Will we be vocal in telling others about His Son and the salvation He offers (1 Thessalonians 1:8)?

Our daily existence as a Christian is eternally more important

---

6. Ibid.

than any game or worldly event.

MINIMIZATION OF RESPONSIBILITY

It is not the Lord's morning; it is the Lord's Day. Our Sundays have long been characterized by at least two services. While this is a tradition, each congregation's leadership decides what is best for each particular group. A second gathering, whether it is an hour-long worship, small group, or service project, provides another opportunity to worship, fellowship and serve, which is advantageous to our spiritual welfare.

Love for God and for our brethren should motivate us to desire to be present when the church meets. James Abram Garfield, our 20th President provides an example of one who had the responsibility of leading the greatest country in the world, who took time to honor God on the Lord's Day.

> In *The Lookout* was a story of how on President Garfield's first Saturday in Washington as President, a member of the Cabinet insisted that a Cabinet meeting must be called at 10 a.m., the following day, to handle a matter that threatened a national crisis. Garfield refused on the ground of another engagement. The Cabinet member insisted. Garfield still refused claiming the other was a prior engagement. The Cabinet member then insisted that the national matter was of such grave importance that the President should break the engagement. Garfield refused. Then the Cabinet member remarked, I should be interested to know with whom you could have an engagement so important that it could not be broken." Garfield replied, "I will be as frank as you are. My engagement is with my Lord to meet him at his house and at his table at 10:30 tomorrow, and I shall be there." The crisis passed. The nation survived. President Garfield had

been faithful to his obligation.[7]

Being absent is usually evidence of other issues. "Those who attend church services irregularly evidence the symptoms of lukewarmness, indifference, selfishness, and love of the world more than the Love of God."[8] A greater effort may be required to be present but where would Jesus be?

CHECKS & BALANCES

As a Christian, attending worship includes:

- Being present because you want to put the Lord first in every aspect of your life (Matthew 6:33).
- Being present because you do not want to forsake the assembly of the saints.
- Being present because you want to encourage your brothers and sisters in the Lord (Hebrews 10:24-25).
- Being present because you want to grow spiritually through the study of the Word of God (1 Peter 2:2).
- Being present because you want to grow closer to other Christians (edification).
- Being present because you want to teach the youth what it means to have closer walk with the Lord.
- Being present because you love the Lord with all of your heart, soul, mind, and strength.
- Being present because you want to encourage young Christians in the faith who are on fire for the Lord because they have not learned that it is okay to miss for

---

7. Leslie Thomas, *Another Hundred Sermons* (Nashville: Gospel Advocate, 1954), 146.

8. Guy N. Woods, *Questions and Answers Vol. II* (Nashville: Gospel Advocate. 1986), 35-36.

all the above reasons.
- Being present because you love to be involved in fellowship with other Christians.
- Being present because you are an important part of the Body of Christ and you are needed.

To properly live our lives pleasing to God, we must have our priorities in proper order to honor God on the Lord's Day, which will enable us to live godly lives between Sundays.

May we think seriously about the need for personal involvement when the church meets. Attending services helps us to put Christ's desires over our own. Our decisions affect others. Be thankful to God for the wonderful example and influence of those who teach us how to live.

QUESTIONS

1. List the items of worship authorized each Sunday for the congregation. For example, Ephesians 5:19; Acts 20:7.
2. List five benefits of being present at the services of the church.
3. What has caused Sunday to be more average in our culture?
4. How can we avoid the temptation to schedule Sunday with other activities?
5. How does my absence from worship affect others?

2

I WILL LIVE BY FAITH

True Christianity is lived out in our daily lives by allowing Christ to live in us. "I have been crucified with Christ. It is no longer I who live, but Christ who lives in me. And the life I now live in the flesh I live by faith in the Son of God, who loved me and gave himself for me" (Galatians 2:20). The Christian walks by faith trusting in God and His Word for direction: "For we walk by faith, not by sight" (2 Corinthians 5:7). Our daily lives between Sundays will be led by a faith that is deep and abiding in Christ.

FAITH EXPLAINED

Hebrews 11:1 is a description of faith: "Now faith is the assurance of things hoped for, the conviction of things not seen for by it the people of old received their commendation. By faith we understand that the universe was created by the word of God, so that what is seen was not made out of things that are visible" (Hebrews 11:1-3 ESV). "As such, faith involves believing that someone else will do something that is not yet visible or that has not yet happened. Thus, to have faith is to relinquish trust in oneself and to put that trust in another."[1]

---

1. Eugene E. Carpenter and Philip W. Comfort, *Holman Treasury of Key Bible Words: 200 Greek and 200 Hebrew Words Defined and Explained* (Nashville, TN: Broadman & Holman Publishers, 2000), 279.

The impala, a medium-sized African antelope, can jump 10 feet high with a distance of 30 feet. Yet it can be kept in a zoo behind a four-foot fence! Why doesn't the impala just jump over the fence? Because, it will not jump when it cannot see where its feet will land. Similarly, faith can be a problem for many people.[2] Faith is not a blind leap in the dark (Romans 1:20). It is believing and following the evidence as presented in the Scriptures. "While we are in the present state, faith supplies the place of direct vision. In the future world we shall have sight—the utmost evidence of spiritual and eternal things, as we shall be present with them, and live in them. Here we have the testimony of God, and believe in their reality, because we cannot doubt his word."[3]

COMPONENTS OF FAITH

The Christian's faith is made up of several components:

1. Knowledge. "So faith comes from hearing, and hearing through the word of Christ" (Romans 10:17). The information in God's Word directs us to establish our faith and live by it.

2. Mental assent. "But when they believed Philip as he preached good news about the kingdom of God and the name of Jesus Christ, they were baptized, both men and women. Even Simon himself believed, and after being baptized he continued with Philip. And seeing signs and great miracles performed, he was amazed" (Acts 8:12-13). The Samaritans "believed" and such belief was translated into their actions.

3. Confidence (trust). "But I received mercy for this reason, that in me, as the foremost, Jesus Christ might

---

2. https://bible.org/illustration/african-impala.

3. Adam Clarke, *Clarke's Commentary*, Vol. 6 (New York: Abingdon Press), 335. Comments on 2 Corinthians 5:7.

display his perfect patience as an example to those who were to believe in him for eternal life" (1 Timothy 1:16). We trust and rely on Christ for our salvation.

4. Obedience. "And the word of God continued to increase, and the number of the disciples multiplied greatly in Jerusalem, and a great many of the priests became obedient to the faith" (Acts 6:7). Obedience describes the action to take and is a key which unlocks our entrance into God's loving favor and life as a Christian.

Belief in the New Testament means trust (Romans 3:20-27); commitment ("and he died for all, that those who live might no longer live for themselves but for him who for their sake died and was raised") (2 Corinthians 5:15), and obedience, "Why do you call me 'Lord, Lord,' and not do what I tell you?" (Luke 6:46). "Faith is whole-souled trust in God's word as true because of the sufficiency of the evidence."[4] "The distinctive feature of faith, in contrast with mere belief, is the element in it of will to action. Belief is an act of the intellect, and faith has been described as 'an act of the intellect commanded by the will.' But faith is more than an act of the intellect, and the will does more than command. Faith is not merely the assent that something is true, it is our readiness to act on what we believe true. Faith is will lured by value into action. Faith is decision."[5]

PUTTING FAITH INTO PRACTICE

In Hebrews 11, inspiration reinforces the fact that faith accepted by God is proved by obedience.

- Abel: "By faith Abel offered unto God a more excellent

---

4. E. J. Carnell, *An Introduction to Christian Apologetics* (Grand Rapids: Eerdmans, 1966), 66.

5. Samuel Thompson's, *A Modern Philosophy of Religion* (Chicago: H. Regnery Company, 1955), 74.

sacrifice…" (11:4).

- Enoch: "By faith Enoch was translated that he should not see death…" (11:5).
- Noah: "By faith Noah…moved with fear, prepared an ark to the saving of his house…" (11:7).
- Abraham: "By faith Abraham, when he was called to go out into a place which he should after receive for an inheritance, obeyed; and he went out…" "By faith he sojourned in the land of promise… "By faith Abraham, when he was tried, offered up Isaac…" (11:8, 9, 17).
- Sarah: "By faith Sarah herself also received strength to conceive seed…" (11:11).
- Moses: "By faith Moses when he became of age, refused to be called the son of Pharaoh's daughter, choosing rather to suffer…" (11:23-28).
- Israelites: "By faith they passed through the Red Sea…" "By faith the walls of Jericho fell down, after they were compassed about seven days" (11:29, 30).
- Rahab: "By faith the harlot Rahab perished not with them that believed not, when she had received the spies with peace" (11:31).

OBEDIENCE

The examples above are models of being obedient to the commands of God and proof of their faith by doing so. "By faith" in each case involved an act of obedience which signified a trust and confidence in God and His commands.

When evidence meets a good heart, faith is developed, followed by obedience. When evidence meets an unbelieving heart, unbelief is the result. Our deeds are an outward physical statement of our inward thoughts. Faith is not opinion. Faith is an intellectual process of receiving something as true on the basis of accurate testimony. Our faith is proven by our action (obedience). The Holy Spirit began and ended the book of Romans with the concept of faith and obedience: "Through Him we have received grace and apostleship for obedience to the faith among all nations for His name…but now made manifest, and by the prophetic Scriptures made known to all nations, according to the commandment of the everlasting God, for obedience to the faith" (Romans 1:5; 16:26).

Between Sundays, the infallible test of our faith includes our works, deeds, and obedience. Walking by faith is being led by the guidance of someone else. We are totally dependent upon Jesus guiding the way and we have total confidence that He is right. We trust Him to lead us in life and into eternity in Heaven.

LIVING BY FAITH AS A CHRISTIAN

Faith is to be manifested through good works. This should be a hallmark of the Christian at all times.

When life is going well, we seem to have no problem with our faith. The career is fulfilling, the family is healthy, financial prosperity is abundant, and life in general is going my way. God is good. Faith is easy to maintain when all is going our way. Between Sundays, there is a major misunderstanding of what it means to live for Jesus. Contrary to what many think, there is a cost of discipleship when it comes to living for Jesus Christ. David Platt has illustrated this concept:

> A nice, middle-class, American Jesus. A Jesus who doesn't mind materialism and who would never call us to give away everything we have. A Jesus who would not expect us to forsake our closest relationships so that he receives all our affection. A Jesus who is fine with nominal devotion that does not infringe on our comforts, because, after all, he loves us just the way we are. A Jesus who wants us to be balanced,

who wants us to avoid dangerous extremes, and who, for that matter, wants us to avoid danger altogether. A Jesus who brings us comfort and prosperity as we live out our Christian spin on the American dream. But do you and I realize what we are doing at this point? We are molding Jesus into our image. He is beginning to look a lot like us because, after all, that is whom we are most comfortable with. And the danger now is that when we gather in our church buildings…in worship, we may not actually be worshiping the Jesus of the Bible. Instead we may be worshiping ourselves.[6]

What happens when we lose our job? The economy curtails our business? A family member develops a serious illness? There is not enough money to cover our bills? We are having serious marital problems? One of the children is having difficulty at school? There is a divorce in our family? Doubts arise, our faith begins to weaken, and we question God about the turn of events in our life.

THE PURPOSE OF GOOD WORKS

Between Sundays, we must put our faith into practice:

- To bring glory to God (Matthew 5:14-16);
- To make us more like Jesus (Acts 10:38);
- To demonstrate living faith (James 2:14-17,20,24);
- To help unbelievers believe (1Peter 2:12);
- To meet urgent needs (Titus 3:14).

In every congregation, there are facilities to be maintained, sick to be tended to, poor to be fed, children to be taught, lost sheep to

---

6. David Platt, *Radical* (Colorado Springs: Multnomah Books. 2010), 13.

be encouraged, souls to be converted, care provided for widows and orphans, the entertaining of strangers, and the sharing our wealth and time (James 5:14-15; Galatians 6:1-2; James 1:27; Romans 12:13; 1 Timothy 6:17-19). Between Sundays, we must think of others as we live our Christianity.

Good works arise out of true faith. True faith in Jesus Christ produces good works. Faith connects us to Christ, and when we are connected to Christ, Christ is living in us, and He is doing good works. And so, true faith in Jesus Christ is extremely important. Good works are not done for me or my neighbor; they are done for God. We want His name honored. We want His kingdom expanded. We want the world to know that God rules, that He sent His Son to save the lost, and that we have the honor of doing good works for Him.

God illustrates this by observing the church as the body of Christ. There is one body and one head (Ephesians 4:1-6). This one body has many members (Romans 12:4). The head directs the body (Ephesians 1:22). The body has ears to hear (Revelation 2:7). The Christian has eyes to see (John 4:35) and a tongue to teach (2 Timothy 2:1-2). Members of the body have shoulders to bear burdens and hands to work.

A Christian is:

- A mind through which Christ thinks.
- A heart through which Christ loves.
- A voice through which Christ speaks.
- A hand through which Christ helps.

Living by faith is taking action in our lives based on the commands of God as we find them recorded in His Word. Two factors make up living by faith:

1. We listen to and obey God's commands.
2. We are doing it because we trust God, not because it makes sense to us.

Remembering to live as Christ directs between Sundays is essential to living by faith!

David Lipscomb believed Christianity was a purposeful life lived in obedience to God.

> The profession of the Christian religion is a vow and an effort to try to live as the word of God directs man to live. "If a man love me, he will keep my word: and my Father will love him, and we will come unto him, and make our abode with him (John 14: 23). I have made a constant and earnest effort, in my teaching the Christian religion to the world and to the church, to impress the absolute necessity of obedience to God. For man to bring himself into harmony with God, the Creator, Preserver, and Ruler of the world, is to love him and gain the highest good and greatest honor that is open to man. To obey and honor God is to bring every true good to man. It is to cut off and save him from every evil. It is the highest and most blessed condition for man.[7]

As we face each day between Sundays, our goal is to face it by faith. Looking through the lens/eyes of Christ (Matthew 6:22), we practice the lifestyle of a follower of Jesus. Prayer is part of the process occurring throughout the day. Honoring God through our work and position in the world is just as important as being the Christlike influence in our family and home life. Our trust in God and the joy of knowing our Savior motivates our obedience. Self-discipline is essential in accomplishing anything. It is easy to drift mindlessly and wander through the day thinking of self and ignoring the opportunities that abound around us. The discipline to notice others and their needs, to stay on course to study, pray, serve, and to be mindful of our purpose requires an intentional lifestyle. We live by faith with

---

7. David Lipscomb, *Salvation From Sin* (Nashville: Gospel Advocate Company, 1950), vii.

life's ups and downs. In our world of distractions, especially in the realm of communication and technology, it is imperative we focus upon what is important and not allow the things of the world to distance us from God. The old cliché "one day at a time" is certainly valid and helpful as we live life. Living between Sundays must be evidence of our trust in God and our desire to obey Him in all things.

Where is your trust? Is it a good job? Is it a "perfect" relationship? Is it money? Is it pleasure? Is it in things? Is it power and control? Is it family? Is it recreation? Is it the Bible? Is it Christ? Is it Heaven? What is your faith doing for you, for God, and for your neighbor between Sundays?

QUESTIONS

1. What are the components of faith? For example: Acts 6:7.
2. What three words describe faith in the New Testament?
3. List some purposes of good works.
4. How do we develop our faith?
5. Why is faith not a "blind leap in the dark"?

3

I WILL HIDE THE WORD IN MY HEART

"Blessed is the man
  who walks not in the counsel of the wicked,
nor stands in the way of sinners,
  nor sits in the seat of scoffers;
but his delight is in the law of the Lord,
  and on his law he meditates day and night" (Psalm 1:1-2).

Between Sundays should be lived out through the Word. The Word of God establishes the Christian's faith. God wants His Word read. It was put in written form for a reason. "Seek and read from the book of the Lord" (Isaiah 34:16). Moses read the book of the law to the people (Exodus 24: 3-8). Israel was required to read the law every Sabbatical year before the men, women, children and strangers, that the law might be heard, learned, and obeyed (Deuteronomy 31:10-12). During the days of Josiah, the law was found and read, resulting in great reforms (2 Kings 22; 23). During Ezra's day, the law was read at length and distinctly before the congregation, with the people standing, listening attentively, worshipping God, and weeping (Nehemiah 8:1-9:3). Jesus recognized people would read God's law. "Have ye not read?" (Matthew 12:3). Jesus Himself read God's Word (Luke 4:16). Paul knew the Bible had to be read in order to understand the mystery (Ephesians 3:3-4). A blessing is placed upon those who read and obey (Revelation 1:3).

GOD'S WORD NEGLECTED

Tragically, in America, we are not reading the Bible as in the past. Strong evidence suggests we do not revere and respect it as the Word of God any longer; we are ignorant of its teaching. As one writer observed at the beginning of the 21st Century: "Biblical illiteracy is rampant even though so many people seem to be getting into the Word. The Bible is the best-selling, least-read, and least-understood book…It's the real dumbing down of America, in that sense."[1] Even more tragic is the fact Christians themselves no longer know the Word. "Regular Bible engagement is both personal and requires discipline. Neither are popular in Western culture today…Too many churchgoers want the benefits of salvation without investing in personally knowing Christ and the abundant life He offers."[2] Belief in the verbal (word for word), plenary (all), inspired (breathed out from God) Word of God (2 Timothy 3:16-17) is an essential faith characteristic of the Christian. Any lesser view of the Bible forfeits a faithful relationship to God and His Word.

The fact that many Bibles are in an unused condition by their owners has serious implications, one of which is that we do not really believe the Bible to be God's breathed out Word.

IMPLICATIONS OF AN UNUSED BIBLE

Have you ever considered the implications of an unused Bible in the life of an individual? Proper growth cannot occur with our Bibles closed (2 Peter 3:18). Precious souls remain lost while our Bibles lay unused (Mark 16:15). The difference between good and evil is not discerned (Hebrews 5:12-14).

On the other hand, consider the implications of an unused Bible in the Church: Proper growth in the congregation does not occur

---

1. David Gibson, "We Revere the Bible . . .We Don't Read It," *Washington Post*, Dec. 9, 2000.

2. http://www.christianpost.com/news/study-most-churchgoers-do-not-read-bible-on-daily-basis-81277/#BWH6a1gVbApAhiLm.99.

(1 Corinthians 3:4-9). Souls are lost because we have smothered the Great Commission by keeping God's Word closed (James 5:19-20). The difference between good and evil is not discerned (doctrinally or morally), which can destroy the unity of the fellowship and faithfulness to God.

> Bible engagement encompasses more than just Bible reading. It measures the extent to which individuals interact with the truth of Scripture and allow it to permeate their thinking and influence their actions…There is a widespread desire among churchgoers to please Jesus, but much less interested in daily wrestling with what pleases Jesus. Instead of Christ being preeminent in the lives of every churchgoer, He is often only the preamble to lives lived apart from biblical truth.[3]

The unused Bible also affects the nation in which we live. "Thus says the Lord: "Cursed is the man who trusts in man and makes flesh his strength, whose heart turns away from the Lord" (Jeremiah 17:5). Noah Webster wrote: "In my view, the Christian religion is the most important and one of the first things in which all children, under a free government ought to be instructed…No truth is more evident to my mind than that the Christian religion must be the basis of any government intended to secure the rights and privileges of a free people."[4]

The Bible reminds us: "Put not your trust in princes, in a son of man, in whom there is no salvation. When his breath departs, he returns to the earth; on that very day his plans perish" (Psalm 146:3-4). "Blessed is the man who trusts in the Lord, whose trust is the Lord" (Jeremiah 17:7).

---

3. Ibid.

4. Noah Webster, 1828, preface, *American Dictionary of the English Language* (San Francisco: Foundation for American Christian Education; Facsimile of 1st edition, 2006).

During the presidency of Ronald Reagan, a proclamation was made designating 1983 as the "Year of the Bible" in the United States. Historically, we have an admirable past. What about the future?

THE BENEFITS OF BIBLE STUDY

Wilbur M. Smith penned several volumes showcasing the abundance of valuable biblical material available to the Bible student. Smith's "Seven things Bible Study will do for you" appeared in his little book *Profitable Bible Study*.[5]

1. **Discovers and convicts us of sin.** "For the word of God is living and active, sharper than any two-edged sword, piercing to the division of soul and of spirit, of joints and of marrow, and discerning the thoughts and intentions of the heart" (Hebrews 4:12; See also: James 1:23-24; 1 John 1:9). The Bible is a mirror into our soul and as we read it, we discover the impurities and sins in our lives and we must act swiftly to remove them by repentance and prayer.

2. **Cleanses us from the pollutions of sin.** "How can a young man keep his way pure? By guarding it according to your word" (Psalm 119:9). Sin sullies our soul and we need the blood of Jesus to wash the sin away (1 John 1:7-10).

3. **Imparts strength.** "...Man does not live by bread alone, but man lives by every word that comes from the mouth of the Lord" (Matthew 4:4). Our spirits need nourishment and God's Word is food for our soul.

4. **Instructs us in what we are to do.** "Everyone then who hears these words of mine and does them will be like a wise man who built his house on the rock. And the

---

5. Wilbur Smith, *Profitable Bible Study* (Boston: Wilde Company, 1939), 11-25.

rain fell, and the floods came, and the winds blew and beat on that house, but it did not fall, because it had been founded on the rock. And everyone who hears these words of mine and does not do them will be like a foolish man who built his house on the sand. And the rain fell, and the floods came, and the winds blew and beat against that house, and it fell, and great was the fall of it" (Matthew 7:24-27). We are to listen to the Word and put the Word into practice, in order to be considered wise.

5. **Provides us with a sword for victory over sin.** God has supplied the armor to stand against Satan and evil. "The sword of the Spirit, which is the word of God" (Ephesians 6:17).

6. **Makes our lives fruitful.** Israel was instructed about how to keep the Word of God before them. This was the key to being faithful to God and receiving His promises. "This Book of the Law shall not depart from your mouth, but you shall meditate on it day and night, so that you may be careful to do according to all that is written in it. For then you will make your way prosperous, and then you will have good success. Have I not commanded you? Be strong and courageous. Do not be frightened, and do not be dismayed, for the Lord your God is with you wherever you go" (Joshua 1:8-9).

7. **Gives us power to pray.** The Christian's weapon, prayer, is an essential component of our daily lives. "If you abide in me, and my words abide in you, ask whatever you wish, and it will be done for you" (John 15:7).

THE BEREANS

In the book of Acts, Luke paints a picture of the Bereans as "more noble" than those in Thessalonica. The Bereans are an excellent example of people who studied between Sundays.

> The brothers immediately sent Paul and Silas away by night to Berea, and when they arrived they went into the Jewish synagogue. Now these Jews were more noble than those in Thessalonica; they received the word with all eagerness, examining the Scriptures daily to see if these things were so. Many of them therefore believed, with not a few Greek women of high standing as well as men.
>
> Acts 17:10-12

The word "noble" is a term applied first to nobility of birth. The word in its secondary sense implies here, nobility of character. They were open-minded about the Scriptures. It is used as a commendation to denote high quality of mind and heart possessed by those in Berea.

What are some things that make for nobility in God's sight?

- **Attitude.** The Bereans "received the word with all eagerness." As on Pentecost, they accepted the truth as it was proclaimed to them (Acts 2:41). Their "eagerness" (stretching the mind forward; anxious to learn) was evident in their persistence in searching the Scriptures. "Blessed are those who hunger and thirst for righteousness, for they shall be satisfied" (Matthew 5:6).

- **Activity.** They were "examining the scriptures daily" (17:11). "Examined" here means "to sift up and down, make careful and exact research as in a legal process."[6] The apostles always affirmed that the doctrines they preached were in accordance with the Old Testament Scriptures (1 Corinthians 15:1-4). The early Christians studied daily (Acts 2:42; 5:42).

- **Accuracy.** The third reason the Bereans were nobler is because they labored for accuracy by determining "if

---

6. *Robertson's Word Pictures*, Vol 3 (Nashville: Broadman, 1930), 274-75.

these things were so," (17:11). They were not content with accepting everything the preacher said (1 John 4:1, 6). They went to the Bible to verify even the teaching of an apostle. They knew a doctrine is true only when God says it is true and were not afraid to change their long-held beliefs if the teaching of God's word demanded such.

- **Accomplishment**. "Many of them therefore believed, with not a few Greek women of high standing as well as men" (17:12). As a result of their conduct (being "noble"), many obeyed the truth. When people search the Scriptures honestly, sincerely, and with an open mind, positive, God-honoring results will come.

STUDYING TOGETHER: BIBLE CLASS AND THE EDUCATIONAL PROGRAM OF THE CHURCH

In his exceptional volume, *Balance*, Ira North noted:

> The educational program of the church offers us the great and glorious opportunity for solid, permanent growth. We urge every member of the local congregation to support the educational program of the church. Give it your time, your attendance, your energy and your help in every way you can. The truth of it is that most of the additions to the congregation come from the educational program, and those that are not converted largely through the educational program of the church must be integrated into such a program or eventually we lose them.[7]

G. Campbell Morgan observed the eternal value of studying the Bible: "The Bible never yields itself to indolence. Of all litera-

---

7. Ira North, *Balance* (Nashville: Gospel Advocate Company, 1983), 70.

ture none demands more diligent application than that of the Divine Library. To that statement, let me hasten to add another. The Bible yields its treasures to honest toil more readily than does any other serious literature."[8] We should seek every opportunity to study God's Word with persistence and tenacity to know more about God and His Will for our lives.

THE IMPORTANCE OF BIBLE CLASS: BE PRESENT

One may ask, "What benefits can be gained by attending a Bible study between Sundays?"

- It helps you put God's kingdom first.
- It helps you gain knowledge about God.
- It helps you possess the mind of Christ.
- It helps you to influence others for good.
- It provides fellowship with other Christians.
- It strengthens your faith in Jesus as Lord.
- It provides nutrition (food) for your soul.
- It helps you to obey God.
- It helps you to be a better guide to your family.
- It helps you to be ready to give an answer to everyone who asks a reason for your faith.
- It helps you to be approved of God.
- It helps you to prepare for the judgment.

THE IMPORTANCE OF BIBLE CLASS: BE PUNCTUAL

The quality of being punctual is a mark of self-discipline and

---

8. G. Campbell Morgan, *The Study and Teaching of the English Bible* (New York: Fleming H. Revell Co., 1910), 78.

a respected mark of an individual. Being late habitually expresses wrong priorities.

If we understand the importance of punctuality in the workplace and other secular appointments, why do we not make the application relative to services of the Church? Should we be "on time" to Bible Class? Worship? The chronically tardy church member is a distraction to those worshipping God, exhibits a lack of self-discipline, and fails to set the proper example to others (Christians & non-Christians).

Are you late for work with the same consistency you are for worship and Bible class? Are your children late to school every day? Would you be tardy for a job interview? We are punctual to occasions which are important to us.

The study of the Bible is a lifetime effort. It is a daily task, a between Sundays task. Study the Word of God "which is able to build you up and to give you the inheritance among all those who are sanctified" (Acts 20:32). Are you approaching the Bible with an open mind? Do you have a passion to know the truth and develop a love for the truth? May we always maintain a fresh and positive attitude toward the Word of God and seek to incorporate it into our everyday lives. "And it shall be with him, and he shall read in it all the days of his life, that he may learn to fear the Lord his God by keeping all the words of this law and these statutes, and doing them" (Deuteronomy 17:19).

QUESTIONS

1. How often did Moses instruct Israel to read the law?
2. Did Paul believe the Bible could be understood?
3. Using 2 Timothy 3:16-17, discuss the inspiration of the Bible.
4. List and apply the seven things Bible study will do for you.
5. What is involved in "examining the scriptures daily" (Acts 17:11)?

4

I WILL LOVE WITH HEART, SOUL, MIND, & STRENGTH

A Peanuts cartoon shows Lucy standing with her arms folded and a stern expression on her face. Charlie Brown pleads, "Lucy, you must be more loving. This world really needs love. You have to let yourself love to make this world a better place." Lucy angrily whirls around and knocks Charlie Brown to the ground. She screams at him, "Look, Blockhead, the world I love. It's people I can't stand."

We all have experienced times we felt this way. Sometimes we are not very loveable people. Despite that, we must love one another the way God teaches us to in His Word. Love may come easy on the Lord's Day, but what about between Sundays? C. S. Lewis acknowledged: "But Divine Gift-love in the man enables him to love what is not naturally lovable; lepers, criminals, enemies, morons, the sulky, the superior and the sneering."[1] In other words, it takes strenuous effort.

THE DOUBLE LOVE COMMANDMENT

> But when the Pharisees heard that he had silenced the Sadducees, they gathered together. And one of them, a lawyer, asked him a question to test him. "Teacher, which is the great commandment in the Law?" And he said to him, "You shall love the Lord your God

---

1. C. S. Lewis, *The Four Loves* (New York: Harcourt Brace, 1988), 128.

with all your heart and with all your soul and with all your mind. This is the great and first commandment. And a second is like it: You shall love your neighbor as yourself. On these two commandments depend all the Law and the Prophets."

Matthew 22:34-40

A parallel treatment of the same concept is found in Mark: "And the scribe said to him, 'You are right, Teacher. You have truly said that he is one, and there is no other besides him. And to love him with all the heart and with all the understanding and with all the strength, and to love one's neighbor as oneself, is much more than all whole burnt offerings and sacrifices.' And when Jesus saw that he answered wisely, he said to him, 'You are not far from the kingdom of God.' And after that no one dared to ask him any more questions" (Mark 12:32-34). In short, God requires total love toward Him and commitment to love our fellow man.

LOVE GOD

In answer to the scribe's question, Jesus quotes: "You shall love the Lord your God with all your heart and with all your soul and with all your might," which is found in Deuteronomy 6:5. This was taught consistently to God's people: "And now, Israel, what does the Lord your God require of you, but to fear the Lord your God, to walk in all his ways, to love him, to serve the Lord your God with all your heart and with all your soul, and to keep the commandments and statutes of the Lord, which I am commanding you today for your good" (Deuteronomy 10:12-13)? David provides an example of exemplifying this love toward God by referencing Josiah. "Before him there was no king like him, who turned to the Lord with all his heart and with all his soul and with all his might, according to all the Law of Moses, nor did any like him arise after him" (2 Kings 23:25).

I WILL LOVE WITH HEART, SOUL, MIND, & STRENGTH 41

AGAPE

Jesus brings together two well-known teachings and forms the basis of devotion toward God. The word here for love is agape. It is a love of commitment, a love that seeks the highest good of others. Agape love drives you to do good for someone, even when you do not want to or feel like it.

> When one is 100% committed to something or to some person, the word describing such an attachment is agape. Even if that devotion is to darkness, to vanities (chief seats, salutations, praises of men), to money, or to lying, it is agape (Psalms 52:3-4; Ecclesiastes 5:10; Luke 11: 43; John 3:19; 12:43). Then, in the opposite direction from a devotion to self, agape is good will and selfless giving even of one's own life to help others. It involves a commitment without thought of gain or loss to the giver, or merit on the part of the receiver.[2]

God desires us. He demands our love and total devotion to Him. We must choose to love and serve Him. This is to be practiced between Sundays. "The relationship of all the Old Testament to the double love commandment shows that there is a hierarchy of law that above all requires one's heart attitude to be correct. If this is absent, obedience to commandments degenerates into mere legalism."[3] Rules without relationship equal rebellion.

APPLICATION

How are we to love God today? Does God expect any less of us? We are to love (agape) God with our: heart, soul, mind, and strength.

---

2. Hugo McCord, *These Things Speak* (Self-published), 128-29.

3. Craig Blomberg, *Matthew* (Vol. 22; The New American Commentary; Nashville: Broadman & Holman Publishers, 1992), 335.

John William McGarvey has written; "He who loves God as required will keep all of God's commandments and he who loves his neighbor will fulfill every obligation to his neighbor. The lawyer went away with the idea not that one specific commandment of God is more important than another, but that the great thing is to have a heart for doing all that God commands."[4]

HEART

With all our heart: the interior, the inner self. This involves a person's thoughts (mind), volition, emotions, and knowledge of right from wrong, conscience. Our thinking must be totally influenced by His thinking. We can know God's thoughts through knowing His Word. "Keep your heart with all vigilance, for from it flow the springs of life" (Proverbs 4:23). Out of the heart we find evidence of each individual's will, desires, passions, affections, perceptions, and thoughts. "For where your treasure is, there your heart will be also" (Matthew 6:21). "The good person out of the good treasure of his heart produces good, and the evil person out of his evil treasure produces evil, for out of the abundance of the heart his mouth speaks" (Luke 6:45).

SOUL

With all our soul: breath of life, life-principle, soul (Romans 12:1-2). "As a deer pants for flowing streams, so pants my soul for you, O God. My soul thirsts for God, for the living God. When shall I come and appear before God?" (Psalm 42:1-2). Christians will give God their body and mind; their all: "I beseech you therefore, brethren, by the mercies of God, that you present your bodies a living sacrifice, holy, acceptable to God, which is your reasonable service. And do not be conformed to this world, but be transformed by the renewing of your mind, that you may prove what is that good and ac-

---

4. J. W. McGarvey, *The New Testament Commentary: Vol 1. Matthew and Mark* (Delight: Gospel Light Publishing, 1968), 193.

ceptable and perfect will of God" (Romans 12:1-2). Our soul is eternal and should not be compromised with worldly allegiance. "For whoever would save his life will lose it, but whoever loses his life for my sake will find it. For what will it profit a man if he gains the whole world and forfeits his soul? Or what shall a man give in return for his soul" (Matthew 16:25-26)?

MIND

With all of our mind: seat of our intellect, our understanding of God, intelligence. It is having the right disposition and attitude toward God. Reason (Isaiah 1:18) is the power to think that God has created within us. Knowledge (Hebrews 10:16) is necessary in order to properly love God and be pleasing to Him. Remembering (memory) is essential for us to love God because it gives us 'recall' of what God has done for us in the past. "I will recount the steadfast love of the Lord, the praises of the Lord, according to all that the Lord has granted us, and the great goodness to the house of Israel that he has granted them according to his compassion, according to the abundance of his steadfast love" (Isaiah 63:7). Paul relayed to the Colossians that our minds are to be linked to Christ. "If then you have been raised with Christ, seek the things that are above, where Christ is, seated at the right hand of God" (Colossians 3:1). Purity of thought will translate into a lifestyle that is pleasing to the Heavenly Father: "Finally, brothers, whatever is true, whatever is honorable, whatever is just, whatever is pure, whatever is lovely, whatever is commendable, if there is any excellence, if there is anything worthy of praise, think about these things" (Philippians 4:8).

STRENGTH

With all our strength: all the energy of our being. This means the call to love God is not only with our physical strength, but also with everything we have available. We are to love Him with all our being, our will, and purpose, conforming our ways to His ways. "All" is repeated four times in Mark 12:30 with the emphasis that our "heart" is our "soul" is our "mind" is our "strength."

God desires the totality of being committed to Him. Love must be a part of our daily lives between Sundays. He wants us to be in fellowship with Him. "God will have no mere part, allow no division or subtraction. Not even the smallest corner is to be closed against God." We demonstrate our love for God through keeping His commandments. This is the love of God (1 John 5:3); this is evidence that we love Jesus (John 14:15). Every facet of our being should be in the control of the Creator. May we say:

> This day do I, with the utmost solemnity, surrender myself to Thee. I renounce all former lords that have had dominion over me; and I consecrate to thee all that I am, and all that I have; the faculties of my mind, the member of my body, my worldly possessions, my time, and my influence over others; to be all used entirely for thy glory, and resolutely employed in obedience to thy commands, as long as thou continues me in life…To thee I leave the management of all events, and say without reserve, "Not my will, but thine be done."[5]

The Ten Commandments also hang on these two laws. The two generic, inclusive commands are sometimes used to sum up the more specific ten. "Love God" sums up the first four, and "love thy neighbor" the last six.

"Since this is God's own commandment, uttered by his own mouth, we here have a psychology of man as it is conceived by man's own Creator who certainly knows man better than man can possibly know himself."[6]

Our love for God must not consist of a compartmentalized ar-

---

5. Philip Doddridge, *The Rise and Progress of Religion in the Soul (1861)*, 251-52.

6. R. C. H. Lenski, *Matthew*, 880.

rangement where we seek to honor God in one area and not in another.

> The core problem isn't the fact that we're lukewarm, halfhearted, or stagnant Christians. The crux of it all is why we are this way, and it is because we have an inaccurate view of God. We see Him as a benevolent Being who is satisfied when people manage to fit Him into their lives in some small way. We forget that God never had an identity crisis. He knows that He's great and deserves to be the center of our lives. Jesus came humbly as a servant, but He never begs us to give Him some small part of ourselves. He commands everything from His followers.[7]

LOVE YOUR NEIGHBOR

The second part of Jesus' answer quotes the Old Testament again: "You shall not take vengeance or bear a grudge against the sons of your own people, but you shall love your neighbor as yourself: I am the Lord" (Leviticus 19:18). The fulfillment of this part of the command begins with loving self. Loving our neighbor is a response to God's love (1 John 4:7). We interact with our neighbors in the world every day. God desires we love others between Sundays. We show love to our neighbor by keeping God's commands (1 John 5:2). "Owe no one anything, except to love each other, for the one who loves another has fulfilled the law. For the commandments, 'You shall not commit adultery, You shall not murder, You shall not steal, You shall not covet,' and any other commandment, are summed up in this word: 'You shall love your neighbor as yourself.' Love does no wrong to a neighbor; therefore, love is the fulfilling of the law" (Romans 13:8-10).

To love is to take a risk.

---

7. Francis Chan, *Crazy Love* (Colorado Springs: Cook, 2008), 20.

> To love at all is to be vulnerable. Love anything and your heart will be wrung and possibly broken. If you want to make sure of keeping it intact you must give it to no one, not even an animal. Wrap it carefully round with hobbies and little luxuries; avoid all entanglements. Lock it up safe in the casket or coffin of your selfishness. But in that casket, safe, dark, motionless, airless, it will change. It will not be broken; it will become unbreakable, impenetrable, irredeemable.[8]

"Jesus' twofold answer should warn Christians against emphasizing either piety for God or social concern at the expense of the other." We are to seek a balance of loving God with our whole being and at the same time maintaining an awareness of our fellow man and his needs between Sundays.

PASS BY OR STOP AND HELP?

The teaching of Jesus in the parable of the good Samaritan (Luke 10:29-37) pertains to the inconsistency of divorcing neighborliness from religion (James 1:22, 26-27). A neighbor is anyone in need whom we can help (John 4:1-30).

The priest and Levite's lack of compassion versus the Samaritan's total involvement in helping his neighbor emphasize the choices we have in our treatment of our fellow man. "For I say to you, that unless your righteousness exceeds the righteousness of the scribes and Pharisees, you will by no means enter the kingdom of heaven" (Matthew 5:20). What is your righteousness like; that of the priest and Levite, or of the Samaritan? Only as we emulate the example of the good Samaritan, can it be said that our righteousness exceeds that of the scribes and Pharisees. Our love for God and for our neighbor is interwoven and influences one another. "Loving God with all of our being will be the determining factor on how we love our neighbor. The extent to

---

8. C. S. Lewis, *The Four Loves* (San Francisco: HarperOne, 2017), 121.

which we love our neighbor will determine how strong our love is for God. "It is only when we love God that man becomes lovable."[9]

The cost of compassion includes: crossing social barriers; taking risks; setting aside busy schedules; and making sacrifices to accomplish the mission (Luke 6:29-30, 34-35).

GOOD QUALITIES OF THE SAMARITAN

Like the Samaritan, between Sundays, we need to be:

- Compassionate (moved to do something).
- Tolerant (help our enemy without bigotry or racism).
- Courageous (feared not return of robbers).
- Helpful (medication, bound up wounds).
- Unselfish (set him on his own beast).
- Generous (paid for his care at the inn).
- Go the second mile (promised additional help if necessary).

Between Sundays, we are to love our spouses, children, parents, teachers, friends, co-workers, our bosses, enemies, strangers, and all others as we love ourselves.

LOVE IS THE CURE FOR HATE

"Love your enemies and pray for those who persecute you, so that you may be sons of your Father who is in heaven. For he makes his sun rise on the evil and on the good, and sends rain on the just and on the unjust" (Matthew 5:44-45). In loving our enemy, we should forgive and let the past go; find common ground and reach out with the active good will that Christ identifies as agape love.

---

9. William Barclay, *The Gospel of Matthew*, vol. 2 (Westminster John Knox Press, 2001), 308.

We have a duty to love God, neighbor, and self. Christianity involves more than just duties to perform, obligations to meet, and rituals to practice, it involves the heart, and this is to permeate our lives between Sundays.

QUESTIONS

1. What is the double love commandment?
2. Where in the Old Testament is the command to love God and neighbor? Why do you think these are both necessary?
3. Which love is described as a commitment that seeks the highest good in others?
4. With what four areas of our being are we to love God? Why is that hard to do in this world?
5. Discuss the differences between the priest, Levite, and the Samaritan.

5

I WILL BE SALT, LIGHT, & LEAVEN

DNA, or deoxyribonucleic acid, is a unique genetic fingerprint found in every cell of the human body. A trace can yield a DNA profile, which is compared to DNA samples from known criminals or other evidence. DNA is the building block for the human body; virtually every cell contains DNA. The DNA in people's blood is the same DNA in their saliva, skin tissue, hair, and bone. Importantly, DNA does not change throughout a person's life. DNA is a powerful investigative tool because, except for identical twins, no two people have the same DNA.

It is likely a fingerprint, footprint, trace of hair, saliva, a thread of clothing or some other DNA will be left to document who was at a crime scene. Criminologists tell us no person enters and exits a room without leaving something of them behind.

Our example is left behind in a similar fashion. You cannot escape being an example to others. Between Sundays, your influence has a powerful reach into other's lives. We are most often unaware of the eyes that are watching our actions or the ears that are listening to our words. We can shape other's thoughts and impressions. It was Thoreau who wrote: "If you would convince a man that he does wrong, do right. But do not care to convince him. Men will believe what they see. Let them see." It is inevitable that, positively or negatively, we will affect the lives of other people.

WHAT IS INFLUENCE?

Influence is described as a direct and intangible means similar to examples, behaviors, and conduct of another. It is the capacity to influence the character, development, or behavior of someone or something. A row of dominoes illustrates this concept: the movement of one affects them all. We have the ability to influence how others think. We have the ability to influence how others feel. We have the ability to influence how others act. The stewardship of influence is about the stewardship of relationships. "For none of us lives to himself, and none of us dies to himself" (Romans 14:7). William J. Bennett recognized that, "We—all of us, but especially the young—need around us individuals who possess a certain nobility, a largeness of soul, and qualities of human experience worth imitating and striving for."

Quality individuals around us contribute to our well-being and help form us into people of character.

IMPORTANCE OF OUR INFLUENCE

- "Be imitators of me, as I am of Christ" (1 Corinthians 11:1).
- "And you became imitators of us and of the Lord, for you received the word in much affliction, with the joy of the Holy Spirit" (1 Thessalonians 1:6).
- "Remember your leaders, those who spoke to you the word of God. Consider the outcome of their way of life, and imitate their faith" (Hebrews 13:7).
- "Brothers, join in imitating me, and keep your eyes on those who walk according to the example you have in us. For many, of whom I have often told you and now tell you even with tears, walk as enemies of the cross of Christ" (Philippians 3:17-18).
- "A disciple is not above his teacher, but everyone when he is fully trained will be like his teacher" (Luke 6:40).

- "Command and teach these things. Let no one despise you for your youth, but set the believers an example in speech, in conduct, in love, in faith, in purity. Until I come, devote yourself to the public reading of Scripture, to exhortation, to teaching. Do not neglect the gift you have, which was given you by prophecy when the council of elders laid their hands on you. Practice these things, immerse yourself in them, so that all may see your progress. Keep a close watch on yourself and on the teaching. Persist in this, for by so doing you will save both yourself and your hearers" (1 Timothy 4:11-16).

The word 'imitate' means, to use as your model; a person who copies the behavior of another in these passages indicates a close resemblance in things that pertain to faithfulness in Christ.

Following the original is certainly the right course. It was Samuel Johnson who wrote:

> Almost every man, if closely examined, will be found to have enlisted himself under some leader whom he expects to conduct him to renown; to have some hero or other, living or dead, in his view, whose character he endeavours to assume, and whose performances he labours to equal. When the original is well chosen and judiciously copied, the imitator often arrives at excellence which he could never have attained without direction; for few are formed with abilities to discover new possibilities of excellence, and to distinguish themselves by means never tried before.

POSITIVE AND NEGATIVE INFLUENCE

Examples of positive influence are found throughout the Bible:

- **Joshua.** "He said, 'Then put away the foreign gods that are among you, and incline your heart to the Lord, the God of Israel.' And the people said to Joshua, 'The Lord our God we will serve, and his voice we will obey.' Israel served the Lord all the days of Joshua, and all the days of the elders who outlived Joshua and had known all the work that the Lord did for Israel" (Joshua 24:23-24, 31).

- **The Thessalonian church.** Paul boasted to other congregations about the church in Thessalonica and how they were a positive influence in their service and work. "We ought always to give thanks to God for you, brothers, as is right, because your faith is growing abundantly, and the love of every one of you for one another is increasing. Therefore we ourselves boast about you in the churches of God for your steadfastness and faith in all your persecutions and in the afflictions that you are enduring" (2 Thessalonians 1:3-4).

Examples of negative influence are also found throughout the Bible:

- **Solomon's wives.** "He had 700 wives, who were princesses, and 300 concubines. And his wives turned away his heart. For when Solomon was old his wives turned away his heart after other gods, and his heart was not wholly true to the Lord his God, as was the heart of David his father" (1 Kings 11:3-4).

- **False teachers.** Paul relayed to Timothy the negative influence of those who pervert God's Word and spread false teaching: "Remind them of these things, and charge them before God not to quarrel about words, which does no good, but only ruins the hearers. Do your best to present yourself to God as one approved, a worker who has no need to be ashamed, rightly handling the word of truth. But avoid irreverent babble, for it will lead people into more and more ungodliness, and their talk will spread like gangrene. Among them are Hymenaeus and Philetus, who have swerved from the truth, saying that the resurrection has already happened. They are upsetting the faith of some. But God's firm foundation stands, bearing this seal: 'The Lord knows those who are his,' and, 'Let everyone who names the name of the Lord depart from iniquity'" (2 Timothy 2:14-19).

SALT, LIGHT, & LEAVEN

You are the salt of the earth, but if salt has lost its taste, how shall its saltiness be restored? It is no longer good for anything except to be thrown out and trampled under people's feet. "You are the light of the world. A city set on a hill cannot be hidden. Nor do people light a lamp and put it under a basket, but on a stand, and it gives light to all in the house. In the same way, let your light shine before others, so that they may see your good works and give glory to your Father who is in heaven.

Matthew 5:13-16

Jesus uses figures of speech (metaphors) to describe our Christian influence in the world. These are essential elements we must practice between Sundays.

SALT

Salt has two primary qualities, to render food more agreeable to taste, and to preserve things.

APPLICATION

"In the biblical world, salt was associated with life due to its uses as a preservative, a purifying agent, and a seasoning. Many of the symbols attached to salt reflect its practical uses. For example, because salt can delay the rotting or decaying process when rubbed into meat, it is a symbol of incorruptibility."[1] The presence of salt makes a difference. There must be immediate contact to avail anything.

Human instruments, Christians, are the greatest preserving influence on the earth. Amazing transformations take place because of the influence of pure Christianity (Colossians 4:5-6). Salty people live by the golden rule and positively influence lives. Salty people preserve society. They are positive influencers; they teach us to connect through sacrifice and self-restraint, not survival of the fittest. They teach us to help our neighbors and share with them rather than find their weaknesses and defeat them.

How can salt lose its effectiveness? It is only when foreign substances are mixed with the pure salt that it loses its power (2 Corinthians 6:14-18). "Most of the salt used in Israel [sic] came from the Dead Sea and was full of impurities. This caused it to lose some of its flavor."[2]

Salt loses its effectiveness when we allow ourselves between Sundays to be influenced by the world and ungodliness.

LIGHT

The world is in darkness and the light of Christ exposes it. "And this is the judgment: the light has come into the world, and people loved the darkness rather than the light because their works were evil. For everyone who does wicked things hates the light and does

---

1. Robert G. Rayburn II, "Salt," ed. John D. Barry, Lazarus Wentz, et al., *The Lexham Bible Dictionary* (Bellingham, WA: Lexham Press, 2014).

2. E.W. Bullinger, *Figures of Speech Used in the Bible* (Grand Rapids: Baker Book House, 1993), 738.

not come to the light, lest his works should be exposed. But whoever does what is true comes to the light, so that it may be clearly seen that his works have been carried out in God" (John 3:19-21). We also find references that teach us that God is light (John 1:5), Christ is light (John 1:1-9), and the Word illuminates (Psalm 119:105).

APPLICATION

There are seven characteristics which should be involved in Christians being the light of the world. In Matthew chapter 5, we find humility, sorrow for personal sin, meekness, a deep-rooted desire to be righteous, mercy, pureness of heart, and the ability to impart the peace of Christ.

> In both these metaphors of the salt and the light, Jesus teaches about the responsibility of Christians in a non-Christian, or sub-Christian, or post-Christian society. He emphasizes the difference between Christians and non-Christians, between the church and the world, and he emphasizes the influences Christians ought to have on the non-Christian environment. The distinction between the two is clear. The world, he says, is like rotting meat. But you are to be the world's salt. The world is like a dark night, but you are to be the world's light. This is the fundamental difference between the Christian and the non-Christian, the church and the world.[3]

We must reflect Christ in all that we do and say between Sundays.

---

3. John Stott: "Four Ways Christians Can Influence the World How we can be salt and light." *Christianity Today*, October 20, 2011. https://www.christianitytoday.com/ct/2011/october/saltlight.html.

LEAVEN

Leaven is "any substance that produces fermentation when added to dough." Leaven is a pervasive influence that modifies something or transforms it for the better or worse.

APPLICATION

Jesus negatively used leaven to highlight the corrupt doctrines of the Pharisees and Sadducees (Matthew 16:6, 11, 12), and Herod (Mark 8:15). "Beware of the leaven of the Pharisees, which is hypocrisy" (Luke 12:1). Paul described how leaven permeates the contents in which it is located: "Do you not know that a little leaven leavens the whole lump? Cleanse out the old leaven that you may be a new lump, as you really are unleavened" (1 Corinthians 5:7). Several examples remind us of the powerful influence of sin: Adam's sin affected the whole race (Romans 5). Achan's sin caused Israel's defeat (Joshua 7). Rehoboam's sin divided the kingdom (1 Kings 12).

A little match can burn a forest. A little water can sink the ship. A little sin can keep the church from being pure.

Jesus used leaven positively to illustrate the power of the kingdom of God and its power to influence for good: "He said therefore, 'What is the kingdom of God like? And to what shall I compare it? It is like a grain of mustard seed that a man took and sowed in his garden, and it grew and became a tree, and the birds of the air made nests in its branches.' And again he said, 'To what shall I compare the kingdom of God? It is like leaven that a woman took and hid in three measures of flour, until it was all leavened'" (Luke 13:18-21). Christians can be a powerful influence between Sundays.

PERSONAL INFLUENCE

In addition to my parents, some of the most influential people in my life were my paternal grandparents. They were "salt of the earth" individuals who never met a stranger and had untold numbers of neighbors, travelers, preachers, and friends sit at their table and share a meal. Honesty, responsibility, helping your neighbor, and reading your Bible were common traits in the days of my grandparents; they knew hard work. My grandfather worked in timber, ran a country grocery store, farmed, and worked to support his family. My grandmother managed the store in addition to raising six children and attending to her parents in their later years. As members of the church, they were continually traveling to gospel meetings in nearby communities providing transportation so many could attend. There was never a question of where they would be on the Lord's Day. Their dedication to the Lord was an example to me from my earliest remembrances.

Influence and example run deep, and we must make sure we are worthwhile, positive, and godly presentations to those around us. Who is your example?

Paul referred to the Corinthian Christians as "letters of recommendation:" "Are we beginning to commend ourselves again? Or do we need, as some do, letters of recommendation to you, or from you? You yourselves are our letter of recommendation, written on our hearts, to be known and read by all. And you show that you are a letter from Christ delivered by us, written not with ink but with the Spirit of the living God, not on tablets of stone but on tablets of human hearts" (2 Corinthians 3:1-3). We are read by all as we interact through the week between Sundays.

As we imitate Christ and those that follow Him, we must remember we are leaving an example through our own steps for someone else. "Fellow-Christians, do let us study the Bible portrait of the humble man. And let us ask our brethren, and ask the world, whether they recognize in us the likeness to the original." "Beloved, I urge you as sojourners and exiles to abstain from the passions of the flesh, which wage war against your soul. Keep your conduct among the Gentiles honorable, so that when they speak against you as evildoers, they may see your good deeds and glorify God on the day of visitation" (1 Peter 2:11-12).

QUESTIONS

1. What does "imitate" mean?
2. Who did Paul say to imitate? Why would he tell them to do that?
3. In Matthew chapter five, what are the characteristics of light in the Christian life?
4. What are some ways we can be "salty Christians?"
5. Think of a time you were unaware of the example you led.

6

I WILL SERVE

Staff members at Ritz-Carlton Hotels can spend up to $2000 to try and resolve a customer's complaint. Even though they have never sold them, Nordstrom is on record having refunded a customer for a set of tires. Businesses know that customer service is key in keeping faithful customers. Business owners understand the "extra mile" service that gets people's attention. My wife, Deanna, and I went into a coffee shop one evening for coffee; they were out of what we wanted. The manager gave us a refund and willingly offered to find a way to get us what we desired, even if he had to go elsewhere to get it. Quality service in the retail and food industry like these instances is probably rare today in most places.

Service in the life of a Christian goes hand in hand with the position and is to be exercised between Sundays. "And if it is evil in your eyes to serve the Lord, choose this day whom you will serve, whether the gods your fathers served in the region beyond the River, or the gods of the Amorites in whose land you dwell. But as for me and my house, we will serve the Lord" (Joshua 24:15). Jesus knew the importance of service when he stated: "If anyone serves me, he must follow me; and where I am, there will my servant be also. If anyone serves me, the Father will honor him" (John 12:26). "For even the Son of Man came not to be served but to serve, and to give his life as a ransom for many" (Matthew 20:28).

A WORTHY EXAMPLE

And when they came to him, he said to them: "You yourselves know how I lived among you the whole time from the first day that I set foot in Asia, serving the Lord with all humility and with tears and with trials that happened to me through the plots of the Jews; how I did not shrink from declaring to you anything that was profitable, and teaching you in public and from house to house, testifying both to Jews and to Greeks of repentance toward God and of faith in our Lord Jesus Christ. And now, behold, I am going to Jerusalem, constrained by the Spirit, not knowing what will happen to me there, except that the Holy Spirit testifies to me in every city that imprisonment and afflictions await me. But I do not account my life of any value nor as precious to myself, if only I may finish my course and the ministry that I received from the Lord Jesus, to testify to the gospel of the grace of God. And now, behold, I know that none of you among whom I have gone about proclaiming the kingdom will see my face again. Therefore I testify to you this day that I am innocent of the blood of all, for I did not shrink from declaring to you the whole counsel of God."

Acts 20:18-28

"Serving the Lord with all humility" (Acts 20:19) was the hallmark of Paul's mission. Serve, as used here, is to perform the duties of a slave.

Paul and the other early disciples of Christ experienced opposition and hardship, which caused many tears and trials. In his comments on Acts 4:25, Alexander Maclaren writes:

> The true position, then, for a man is to be God's slave. The harsh, repellent features of that wicked institu-

tion assume an altogether different character when they become the features of my relation to Him. Absolute submission, unconditional obedience, on the slave's part; and on the part of the Master complete ownership.[1]

A slave is subjected to His Lord and Master. In the case of Christians, we serve our Lord Jesus Christ. "All" constitutes the full quality or extent, the idea of complete.

"Humility" is the recognizing and accepting of our rightful place of subordination to, and dependency upon God. Humility is that quality which is the opposite of pride. Jesus acknowledged: "What comes out of a person is what defiles him. For from within, out of the heart of man, come evil thoughts, sexual immorality, theft, murder, adultery, coveting, wickedness, deceit, sensuality, envy, slander, pride, foolishness. All these evil things come from within, and they defile a person" (Mark 7:20-23). "Humility is honestly assessing ourselves in light of God's holiness and our sinfulness."[2] The Bible stresses the necessity of humility in our lives. "All these things my hand has made, and so all these things came to be, declares the Lord. But this is the one to whom I will look: he who is humble and contrite in spirit and trembles at my word" (Isaiah 66:2). "Clothe yourself with humility, for God gives grace to the humble. Humble yourselves under God" (I Peter 5:5,6).

CRUCIFIXION OF SELF

An important key to developing into servants, who emulate the perfect example of Jesus, is the crucifixion of self. "I have been crucified with Christ. It is no longer I who live, but Christ who lives in me. And the life I now live in the flesh I live by faith in the Son of God,

---

1. Alexander Maclaren, *Expositions of Holy Scripture* (Grand Rapids: Baker, 1982), 169.

2. C.J. Mahaney, *Humility: True Greatness* (Colorado Springs: Multnomah, 2005), 22.

who loved me and gave himself for me" (Galatians 2:20).

We are to go through a transformation (metamorphosis) and put to death the old way of life and put on the new way of Christian living. "But that is not the way you learned Christ! — assuming that you have heard about him and were taught in him, as the truth is in Jesus, to put off your old self, which belongs to your former manner of life and is corrupt through deceitful desires, and to be renewed in the spirit of your minds, and to put on the new self, created after the likeness of God in true righteousness and holiness" (Ephesians 4:20-24). We must present our new selves between Sundays. In order to do that, we work to eliminate habits and practices that are not Christ-like in our everyday lives.

The application of the crucifixion of self is expanded upon by Paul to the Colossians:

> If then you have been raised with Christ, seek the things that are above, where Christ is, seated at the right hand of God. Set your minds on things that are above, not on things that are on earth. For you have died, and your life is hidden with Christ in God. When Christ who is your life appears, then you also will appear with him in glory. Put to death therefore what is earthly in you: sexual immorality, impurity, passion, evil desire, and covetousness, which is idolatry. On account of these the wrath of God is coming. In these you too once walked, when you were living in them. But now you must put them all away: anger, wrath, malice, slander, and obscene talk from your mouth. Do not lie to one another, seeing that you have put off the old self with its practices and have put on the new self, which is being renewed in knowledge after the image of its creator. Here there is not Greek and Jew, circumcised and uncircumcised, barbarian, Scythian, slave, free; but Christ is all, and in all. Put on then, as God's chosen ones, holy and beloved, compassionate hearts, kindness, humility,

meekness, and patience, bearing with one another and, if one has a complaint against another, forgiving each other; as the Lord has forgiven you, so you also must forgive. And above all these put on love, which binds everything together in perfect harmony.

Colossians 3:1-14

The change we experience in conversion gets us prepared for servanthood. We now put our energies into serving others rather than serving self and our sinful desires.

GOING THE SECOND MILE

In New Testament times, Roman couriers were authorized to press into service any available person or beast for transportation of official documents, but they could not compel a citizen to go further than one mile. Citing this practice, Jesus is saying, "Don't go a mile with bitter and obvious resentment. Go two miles with cheerfulness and good grace." This text is a lesson on attitude; we should live with the mindset of the second mile. "You have heard that it was said, 'An eye for an eye and a tooth for a tooth.' But I say to you, do not resist the one who is evil. But if anyone slaps you on the right cheek, turn to him the other also. And if anyone would sue you and take your tunic, let him have your cloak as well. And if anyone forces you to go one mile, go with him two miles. Give to the one who begs from you, and do not refuse the one who would borrow from you" (Matthew 5:38-42).

FIRST MILE - OBLIGATION

"And whoever compels you to go one mile, go with him two" (Matthew 5:42). As we consider Jesus' words, we need to remember that Palestine in the days of Jesus was an occupied country. Rome enforced its rule over the people of Israel by maintaining garrisons of Roman soldiers stationed throughout the country. According to

Roman law, a Roman soldier could require a Jewish citizen to carry his pack for him for a distance of one mile. The law obligated them to this first mile of servanthood. A Biblical example of this is Simon of Cyrene (Matthew 27:32), the man who was made to carry the cross of Jesus. There are two ways to obey: (1) grudging acceptance or (2) graciously and cheerfully. Grudging acceptance is like the little boy who was told to go sit in the corner and as he sat there with his arms crossed he said, "I may be sitting on the outside, but I am standing on the inside." Our attitude needs to display the obedient condition of our heart, gracious and cheerful.

SECOND MILE - HEART

In the Old Testament, Abraham's servant who was sent to find a wife for Isaac finds Rebekah, who shines as an example of one who went the second mile in serving.

> Then the servant ran to meet her and said, "Please give me a little water to drink from your jar." She said, "Drink, my lord." And she quickly let down her jar upon her hand and gave him a drink. When she had finished giving him a drink, she said, "I will draw water for your camels also, until they have finished drinking." So she quickly emptied her jar into the trough and ran again to the well to draw water, and she drew for all his camels.
>
> Genesis 24:17-20

Watering camels was no small task. Camels can drink up to 30 gallons of water at a time.

We usually do not operate on the premise of doing more without expecting anything in return. Many would rather accomplish the smallest amount of labor while anticipating a much bigger return in remuneration. Serving as a slave to God does not come with the idea that we can do the least and gain the most.

In going the second mile, you will be twice as inconvenienced. You will have to walk back two miles to your start. You will be twice as tired. You will have double the time to make up. Your journey becomes one of the heart, serving others and ultimately Christ. It displays our free choice and our unique nature. We exhibit love for our neighbor. It surprises others in that it provides more than was expected. It also enables us to learn not to count the small troubles of life a burden.

First mile things are obligations, ordinary things, but the second mile is an opportunity. The Lord is teaching that as you and I go down the road of life between Sundays, we are to look at the tasks we are given—even those that seem unfair, as opportunities to serve others cheerfully as we reflect the love of Christ.

DORCAS

In the New Testament Dorcas stands out as one that went the second mile in her service:

> Now there was in Joppa a disciple named Tabitha, which, translated, means Dorcas. She was full of good works and acts of charity. In those days she became ill and died, and when they had washed her, they laid her in an upper room. Since Lydda was near Joppa, the disciples, hearing that Peter was there, sent two men to him, urging him, "Please come to us without delay." So Peter rose and went with them. And when he arrived, they took him to the upper room. All the widows stood beside him weeping and showing tunics and other garments that Dorcas made while she was with them. But Peter put them all outside, and knelt down and prayed; and turning to the body he said, "Tabitha, arise." And she opened her eyes, and when she saw Peter she sat up. And he gave her his hand and raised her up. Then calling the saints and widows, he presented her alive. And it became known

throughout all Joppa, and many believed in the Lord.

Acts 9:36-42

What can we learn from this wonderful Christian lady? The sister's devotion: Her attitude and works remind us of Christ and His service to others. Her deeds: "Full of good works" (9:36). The widows were recipients of her benevolence. Her death: "She became ill and died" (9:37). The death of Dorcas left a void among the disciples and those in the community. Those who were mourning her death attested to her good deeds.

> The rule for all of us is perfectly simple. Do not waste your time bothering whether you love your neighbor; act as if you did. As soon as we do this we find one of the great secrets. When you are behaving as if you loved someone, you will presently come to love him. If you injure someone you dislike, you will find yourself disliking him more. If you do him a good turn, you will find yourself disliking him less... The difference between a Christian and a worldly man is not that the worldly man has only affections or likings and the Christian has only charity. The worldly man treats certain people kindly because he likes them; the Christian, trying to treat everyone kindly, finds himself liking more and more people as he goes on – including the people he could not even have imagined himself liking at the beginning.[3]

Meaningful significance is found in serving others. Jesus Christ was the ultimate example of service. Many misunderstand what is really significant in this life.

True Christian service is the giving of self, our resources, money, time, food, clothing; all that we have been given.

---

3. C. S. Lewis, *Mere Christianity* (New York: Macmillan, 1958), 101-2.

We must conform our mind to that of Christ and strengthen our attitudes about serving. The obligation of going the first mile is because of our love of God and Christ our Savior. The second mile walk includes that which is in the first as well as a love for our neighbors. We must be willing to go the extra distance between Sundays in our service to others using opportunities to teach the message of Christ and salvation through our words, actions, and influence.

"For I have given you an example, that you also should do just as I have done to you. Truly, truly, I say to you, a servant is not greater than his master, nor is a messenger greater than the one who sent him. If you know these things, blessed are you if you do them" (John 13:15-18).

Are you a servant in the capacity that Jesus exemplifies between Sundays?

QUESTIONS

1. In Acts 20:18-27, what are some of Paul's characteristics that stand out in his service?
2. What is involved with crucifying self?
3. How does humility relate to serving others?
4. Why did Jesus say for us to go the second mile?
5. List some examples of ways you can serve.

7

I WILL PRACTICE THE GOLDEN RULE

> So whatever you wish that others would do to you,
> do also to them, for this is the Law and the Prophets.
>
> Matthew 7:12

The golden rule is known worldwide. It is one of the most well-known statements of Jesus Christ, and it is the least practiced. In the Sermon on the Mount, we have principles that pertain to our relationship with God and our fellow man. We need to spend more time applying these teachings in our lives between Sundays. John R.W. Stott discusses the Christian counter-culture and how relationships are also included: "…The Christian community is, in essence, a family, God's family. Probably the two strongest elements in our Christian consciousness are an awareness of God as our Father and of our fellow-Christians as our brothers and sisters through Christ, although at the same time we can never forget our responsibility to those outside the family whom we long to see brought in."[1]

IT'S NOT ABOUT ME

Jesus was all about others, not Himself. Thinking of others is core Christianity. This concept is often lost in our current cultural at-

---

1. John R. W. Stott, *The Message of the Sermon on the Mount* (Downers Grove, IL: Inter-Varsity Press, 1985), 192.

titude of "it's all about me." David McCullough Jr., an English teacher at Wellesley High School in Massachusetts gave the commencement address a few years ago and was very direct in relaying to the students a very timely and blunt message: "You're not special."

> Yes, you've been pampered, cosseted, doted upon, helmeted, bubble-wrapped. Yes, capable adults with other things to do have held you, kissed you, fed you, wiped your mouth, wiped your bottom, trained you, taught you, tutored you, coached you, listened to you, counseled you, encouraged you, consoled you and encouraged you again. You've been nudged, cajoled, wheedled and implored. You've been feted and fawned over and called sweetie pie. Yes, you have. And, certainly, we've been to your games, your plays, your recitals, your science fairs. Absolutely, smiles ignite when you walk into a room, and hundreds gasp with delight at your every tweet. Why, maybe you've even had your picture in the Townsman! And now you've conquered high school… and, indisputably, here we all have gathered for you, the pride and joy of this fine community, the first to emerge from that magnificent new building… But do not get the idea you're anything special. Because you're not. As you commence, then, and before you scatter to the winds, I urge you to do whatever you do for no reason other than you love it and believe in its importance… Resist the easy comforts of complacency, the specious glitter of materialism, the narcotic paralysis of self-satisfaction. Be worthy of your advantages. And read… read all the time… read as a matter of principle, as a matter of self-respect. Read as a nourishing staple of life. Develop and protect a moral sensibility and demonstrate the character to apply it. Dream big. Work hard. Think for yourself. Love everything you love, everyone you love, with all your might. And

do so, please, with a sense of urgency, for every tick of the clock subtracts from fewer and fewer; and as surely as there are commencements there are cessations, and you'll be in no condition to enjoy the ceremony attendant to that eventuality no matter how delightful the afternoon.[2]

THE OPTIMISTIC RULE

The golden rule is based upon the absolute best that someone has to offer: It is optimistic. It is not, "do to others as they do to you" or "do to others when they do to you."

The golden rule is a positive statement by Jesus. He is saying to not wait for someone to do good for us, but that we should do it for him or her first. There are statements many consider a form of the golden rule; however, most of those statements set forth a negative connotation, whereas Jesus' rule is positive and demands action. For example, in the Old Testament Apocrypha: "And what thou thyself hatest, do to no man" (Tobit 4:15). Rabbi Hillel stated: "What is hateful to you, do not do to anyone else. This is the whole law; all the rest is only commentary" (Talmud: Shabbath 31a).

The teaching of the Old Law forms the foundation of the golden rule spoken by Christ. "But you shall love your neighbor as yourself: I am the Lord" (Leviticus 19:18 NLT). "Do to others whatever you would like them to do to you. This is the essence of all that is taught in the law and the prophets."

In our daily lives, between Sundays, Jesus commands us to take the initiative. Thomas B. Warren observed:

> "Go, do to your neighbor what you would that he should to unto you." This comes out as meaning, "It is not enough to merely refrain from robbing your neighbor; you should give to him what he deserved-

---

2. "It's All About Me Right," https://theswellesleyreport.com/2012/06/wellesley-high-grads-told-youre-notspecial/.

ly needs." Do not merely not harm your neighbor; rather, do him good. And all of this is to be done out of a pure love for both God and neighbor. One loves his neighbor—in the highest sense—in that he truly loves God, and out of that love sees the intrinsic value both of himself and of his neighbor.[3]

NEGATIVE FORM

The golden rule in negative form implies there is no action required of an individual. The concept is that one should refrain from certain things or actions. In other words: "A man could satisfy the negative form of the rule by simple inaction."[4] Avoid relationships and contact with people and one can fulfill the negative version of the rule. "If we put ourselves sensitively into the place of the other person and wish for him what we would wish for ourselves, we would be never mean, always generous; never harsh, always understanding; never cruel, always kind."[5] We must learn to walk in one another's shoes.

"It is one thing to say, 'I must not injure people; I must not do to them what I would object to their doing to me.' That, the law can compel us to do. It is quite another thing to say, 'I must go out of my way to help other people and to be kind to the, as I would wish them to help and to be kind to me.' That, only love can compel us to do."[6]

NOT RECIPROCAL

This is not a reciprocal relationship. You give me a gift; I give you one back. Many play this game of repaying others for what they

---

3. Thomas B. Warren, *The Book of Matthew* (Memphis: Getwell Church of Christ, 1988), 259.

4. William Barclay, *The Gospel of Matthew, vol. 1*. The Daily Study Bible (Philadelphia: Westminster, 1958), 279.

5. Stott, *Sermon on the Mount*, 192.

6. Barclay, *Matthew*, 280.

give. The golden rule does not operate this way. It is doing, without expecting anything in return. It is our way of life. Our hope and prayer are that others will be doing the same and the beauty of Jesus' command is fulfilling the law and prophets: living out the example of Christ. We are to be doers and not hearers only (James 1:22) and emulate Jesus as He went about doing good (Acts 10:38). There is unselfishness and action presented in the golden rule.

A RULE OF LOVE

God's way teaches us to give all without expecting anything in return. *The Message* captures this idea: "Here is a simple, rule-of-thumb guide for behavior: Ask yourself what you want people to do for you, then grab the initiative and do it for them. Add up God's Law and Prophets and this is what you get." This same principle is applicable to us today: "Do not think that I have come to abolish the Law or the Prophets; I have not come to abolish them but to fulfill them" (Matthew 5:17). Paul applies the teaching of the Old Testament and the words of Christ by stating: "Owe no one anything, except to love each other, for the one who loves another has fulfilled the law. For the commandments, 'You shall not commit adultery, You shall not murder, You shall not steal, You shall not covet,' and any other commandment, are summed up in this word: 'You shall love your neighbor as yourself.' Love does no wrong to a neighbor; therefore, love is the fulfilling of the law" (Romans 13:8-10). The golden rule states to love your neighbor as yourself.

LOVING OUR ENEMIES

In the context of Luke's record, the golden rule follows instructions on how to treat our enemies: love them.

> But I say to you who hear, Love your enemies, do good to those who hate you, bless those who curse you, pray for those who abuse you. To one who strikes

you on the cheek, offer the other also, and from one who takes away your cloak do not withhold your tunic either. Give to everyone who begs from you, and from one who takes away your goods do not demand them back. And as you wish that others would do to you, do so to them.

Luke 6:27-31

Christ reminds us that anyone can return good for good (Matthew 5:46-48). It was the Apostle Peter who wrote:

Finally, all of you, have unity of mind, sympathy, brotherly love, a tender heart, and a humble mind. Do not repay evil for evil or reviling for reviling, but on the contrary, bless, for to this you were called, that you may obtain a blessing. For "Whoever desires to love life and see good days, let him keep his tongue from evil and his lips from speaking deceit; let him turn away from evil and do good; let him seek peace and pursue it. For the eyes of the Lord are on the righteous, and his ears are open to their prayer. But the face of the Lord is against those who do evil.

1 Peter 3:8-12

Stephen exemplified the forgiveness of Christ toward his enemies just before dying: "And falling to his knees he cried out with a loud voice, "Lord, do not hold this sin against them" (Acts 7:60).

GOD'S LOVE FOR MAN REFLECTED IN THE GOLDEN RULE

The golden rule reflects man's love for God. We are not given what we deserve.

> For while we were still weak, at the right time Christ died for the ungodly. For one will scarcely die for a righteous person—though perhaps for a good person one would dare even to die—but God shows his love for us in that while we were still sinners, Christ died for us. Since, therefore, we have now been justified by his blood, much more shall we be saved by him from the wrath of God. For if while we were enemies we were reconciled to God by the death of his Son, much more, now that we are reconciled, shall we be saved by his life. More than that, we also rejoice in God through our Lord Jesus Christ, through whom we have now received reconciliation.
>
> Romans 5:6-11

God displays the golden rule when dealing with us by giving us love, grace, mercy and forgiveness when we deserve His wrath upon us, our punishment, and death.

WHAT DO WE SEEK FROM OTHER PEOPLE?

Between Sundays we experience many of the same needs and desires as those around us in the world. We want people to:

- **Like Us.** This is a common desire of most everyone. We simply want to be accepted and liked. The opposite of being liked is sad: "Look to the right and see: there is none who takes notice of me; no refuge remains to me; no one cares for my soul" (Psalm 142:4). There is a peace of mind and a feeling of belonging when we are liked.
- **Overlook Our Faults and Failings and Forgive.** A common denominator among all people is the fact we all have faults. Everyone commits sin. Our actions toward each other regarding sin are often inconsistent.

When Jesus said: "Let him who is without sin among you be the first to throw a stone at her" (John 8:7), he was exposing the hypocrisy of the accusers of the woman caught in adultery. We should be fulfilling "Be kind to one another, tenderhearted, forgiving one another, as God in Christ forgave you" (Ephesians 4:32).

- **Show Appreciation.** After Jesus had cleansed the ten lepers, one returned, who was a Samaritan, and thanked him. The words of the Lord: "Were not ten cleansed? Where are the nine?" (Luke 17:17), should serve as a reminder to always be thankful and appreciative to others for their work, kindness, generosity, benevolence, concern, and love.

- **Give Us the Benefit of the Doubt.** "Love bears all things, believes all things, hopes all things, endures all things" (1 Corinthians 13:7). The idea of giving others the 'benefit of the doubt' is to believe something good about someone, rather than something bad, when you have the possibility of doing either. This is why Paul commands believers to do the contrary: to focus on the positive. "Finally, brothers, whatever is true, whatever is honorable, whatever is just, whatever is pure, whatever is lovely, whatever is commendable, if there is any excellence, if there is anything worthy of praise, think about these things and to think the best about others, especially those of the household of faith" (Philippians 4:8).

To receive these gifts from others, we must first give them ourselves.

Our Christian lives between Sundays revolve around relationships: with God, Christ, and then our neighbors.

There are implications of applying the golden rule to ourselves that are life changing:

- It forces us to think of others continually, trying to put ourselves in their place.
- It leads us to study ourselves and our own real needs.
- It makes us brotherly, placing the lowest man on the same plane of desire with ourselves.
- It turns us from the past (what we can do for others) and toward the future (what we want others to do for us).
- It requires our deepest nature to be the guide of action, identifying us at once with whatever we do, making us real and sincere.

The golden rule is intended to motivate us to do good works and keep us from putting ourselves at the center of everything. "After all, the law was not meant to be praised, it was meant to be practiced. Our Lord did not preach the Sermon on the Mount in order that you and I might comment upon it, but in order that we might carry it out."[7] Utilizing the golden rule in all of our relationships will take our character to a higher level. Our interactions with others between Sundays offers us the chance to practice the golden rule. The employer and the employee; the elder and the preacher; the elders and the deacons; the youth and the elderly; the teacher and the student; those in public office and the citizens; the husband and the wife; the parents and the children; friend to friend; neighbor to neighbor; Christian to Christian. Jesus' wisdom applied will solve our relational problems and show the world the high standard of conduct that comes from God. Between Sundays, this mandate should forever be impressed upon our minds and hearts.

QUESTIONS

1. In what way is the Golden Rule a rule of love?

---

7. D. Martin Lloyd Jones, *Studies in Sermon on the Mount*, vol. 2 (Grand Rapids: Eerdmans, 1974), 211.

I WILL PRACTICE THE GOLDEN RULE

2. What other verses in the Bible remind you of this verse?
3. What are some applications of the Golden Rule?
4. Are we taught to do unto others as they have or will probably do unto us? What is the difference between this application and what Jesus actually teaches?
5. Is there any suggestion in the verse that you should wait for something to happen to you before you do good to others?

8

I WILL WALK USING A MORAL COMPASS

The New Testament is the pattern for our work, worship, plan of salvation, and lifestyle (Colossians 3:17). Between Sundays, living the Christian life requires diligence, dedication, devotion, and complete submission to the King of kings. When we obey the Gospel of Christ, we are to deny the ungodly and worldly traits of our old life and move forward developing the fruit of the Spirit (Galatians 5:22-23). Living for God based upon our love for Him will direct our lifestyle.

Individuals must be taught they need Jesus and faith in the God who created them. In coming to know and love God, people will be ready to surrender themselves to God's way of living holy and righteously.

WHICH STANDARD APPLIES?

Competing worldviews present an array of options as to the lifestyle one chooses to live. An objective standard of morality, however, is essential for everyone to be on the same page.

> Every society has a structure of systems that either influences or coerces behavior. Eventually, societies move to legislate and regulate behavior in order to align the society with what is commonly, or at least largely, considered morally right and wrong. Civili-

I WILL WALK USING A MORAL COMPASS 79

zation could not survive without a system of moral controls and influences.[1]

Consider the following criteria that falls short of the objective standard for us today. The Old Testament law does not qualify as our standard today since we are under the New Testament (Colossians 2:14). Following the majority of the world fails to meet God's agenda (Exodus 23:2). Our love and respect for our parents must not serve as a template for how we live our lives (Matthew 10:34-37). Preachers and teachers who have a powerful influence in our lives must not be the standard, for they are fallible people (2 Corinthians 11:13-15). Catechisms, creeds and traditions of men are not God's inspired Word and therefore must not be the basis of our morality (Mark 7:3-7). Our own conscience (Acts 23:1; 24:16; 26:9-11), and our human wisdom fail miserably when compared to God's wisdom (Proverbs 14:12). A common misconception is to allow our feelings to shape who we are and how we live, but God's Word says: "Whoever trusts in his own mind is a fool, but he who walks in wisdom will be delivered" (Proverbs 28:26).

Francis Schaeffer was correct when he wrote:

> If there is no absolute moral standard, then one cannot say in a final sense that anything is right or wrong. By absolute we mean that which always applies, that which provides a final or ultimate standard. There must be an absolute if there are to be morals, and there must be an absolute if there are to be real values. If there is no absolute beyond man's ideas, then there is no final appeal to judge between individuals and groups whose moral judgments conflict. We are merely left with conflicting opinions. [2]

---

1. Albert Mohler, *We Cannot Be Silent* (Nashville: Nelson Books, 2015), 119.

2. Francis Schaeffer, *How Then Should We Live?: The Rise and Decline of Western Thought and Culture: The Complete Works of Francis A. Schaeffer Vol 1*

Christianity is the religion of Divine authority. To be pleasing to God, man must be submissive to God's Will for him.

OUR CULTURE

> The current culture is characterized by anything but a devotion to and respect for Christianity. Rather than honoring God as Creator and seeking to base our behavior upon His standard, people go to great lengths to avoid mentioning God and to ridicule and scorn those who do so. Sinful behavior is no longer shunned but embraced. Tolerance is king, except when it comes to those who are religious. Absolute truth is rejected in favor of relativism, and in no place is this truer than when it comes to moral behavior. [3]

Assumptions twist and slant the truth, convincing us they are the truth. Even though our assumptions may directly oppose the Bible, we find difficulty convincing ourselves they are wrong. Notice a few common cultural assumptions pertaining to morality.

The voice of culture offers several perspectives that are in opposition to the biblical concept of man: "Self is number one." It is reasoned that we should always look out for ourselves and think about what is best for us. God's way teaches us to put God first, others second, and self last (Matthew 22:37-39). "I can't help myself." People no longer take personal responsibility for their actions. God teaches us He will judge us for what we do (2 Corinthians 5:10). "No one can claim to know the truth." If someone claims to know the truth, then they are labeled as intolerant, arrogant, and bigoted. Jesus said, "And you shall know the truth and the truth shall set you free" (John 8:32). "All social and moral values are relative" and "the church must keep up with the times." Ethics, morals and values are absolute, constant,

---

(Wheaton: Crossway, 1982), 166.

3. Chad Ramsey, "Living in a Post-Christian Culture," *Gospel Advocate*, Feb 2013.

and fixed in scripture by God (2 Timothy 3:16-17; 2 Peter 1:3).

Is the Bible relative to today's moral questions? Not only is it relative, it is the ultimate authority. Albert Mohler has reasoned: "Moral relativism and the rejection of absolute truth now shape the modern post-Christian mind. Indeed, relativism is virtually taken for granted, at least as an excuse for overthrowing theistic truth claims and any restrictive morality."[4]

Each individual Christian must devote and dedicate his/her life as a sacrifice to God. Between Sundays, we will present our bodies as living sacrifices, only when we come to know and appreciate the price with which we were purchased. "Or do you not know that your body is a temple of the Holy Spirit within you, whom you have from God? You are not your own, for you were bought with a price. So glorify God in your body" (1 Corinthians 6:19-20).

OUR CHOICES

Moses is an example of one who chose to forfeit a life of luxury, ease, power, and wealth in order to serve God. "By faith Moses, when he was grown up, refused to be called the son of Pharaoh's daughter, choosing rather to be mistreated with the people of God than to enjoy the fleeting pleasures of sin. He considered the reproach of Christ greater wealth than the treasures of Egypt, for he was looking to the reward" (Hebrews 11:24-26).

The Christian is to be able to discern good and evil and know the difference between right and wrong, worldly and godly (Hebrews 5:12-14). Even though the world surrounds us, we must be careful not to be influenced by it. As children of God we are to hate evil (Romans 12:9).

Why do Christians choose worldliness over spirituality? One reason may be failure to properly evaluate life; having never tried to reach one's potential in Christian living. Another reason is indifference. There are many who have no interest in spirituality. We might

---

4. http://www.albertmohler.com/2015/12/07/relativity-moral-relativism-and-the-modern-age/.

also consider that some do not want to pay the price; that is, to give up things that prevent us from a relationship with God and Jesus Christ. We must be willing to make sacrifices for our spiritual nature. Many are led and influenced by culture, as we have noted; the free will of man is key in the choices we make, but the Bible must be the standard of our influence.

WE CAN KNOW

We are not abandoned to find our way morally without guidance from God. As Francis Schaeffer observed: "without absolutes, morals as morals cease to exist, and Humanistic man starting from himself has failed to find the absolute. But because the God of the Bible is there, real morals exist. Within this framework I can say one action is right and another wrong, without talking nonsense."[5]

God has given man the intellect (reasoning ability) and the information (Bible) to differentiate between good and evil. We can know what sin is (1 John 3:4), and we can know that all sin is disobedience to the will of God (Revelation 21:8). God's indignation toward immorality is clear: "It is a fearful thing to fall into the hands of the living God" (Hebrews 10:31). The fact remains that immorality will never compare with morality (Psalm 1).

CALL TO ACTION

The application of Biblical morality is necessary for us to live out our faith. Times change, new customs evolve, and standards of morality change. Society accepts behavior today that it would not tolerate yesterday.

> We cannot understand our times without looking honestly at the moral hurricane sweeping across our culture, leaving very little untouched, if not radically

---

5. Francis Schaeffer, *The God Who Is There*, *The Complete Works of Francis A. Schaeffer Vol 1* (Wheaton: Crossway, 1982), 117.

changed, in its wake…we cannot be silent because we know that Jesus Christ is Lord and that he came to save us from our sins. We cannot rightly tell people about the gospel of Jesus Christ if we do not speak rightly about sin and its consequences. [6]

The Christian lives a life devoted to Christ and strives to exemplify that example in word and action. This sets us apart from the world when it comes to our lifestyle. "O Lord, I know the way of man is not in himself; it is not in man who walks to direct his own steps" (Jeremiah 10:23).

CHRISTIANS & THE WORLD

Do not love the world or the things in the world. If anyone loves the world, the love of the Father is not in him. For all that is in the world—the desires of the flesh and the desires of the eyes and pride of life—is not from the Father but is from the world. And the world is passing away along with its desires, but whoever does the will of God abides forever.

1 John 2:15-17

Between Sundays, as we studied in a previous chapter, we are to be salt, light and leaven seeking to influence the world for Christ. Children of God must stand strong in our convictions and not allow the world to dominate and influence our lives.

THE LUST: DESIRE OF THE FLESH

The word translated 'lust' means, strong desires of any kind. It is also used to describe those actions and attitudes that are inconsistent with the will of God (Romans 13:14). Lust is: deceitful (Ephesians

---

6. Albert Mohler, *We Cannot Be Silent* (Nashville: Nelson Books, 2015), xvi-xvii.

4:22), foolish, harmful (1 Timothy 6:9), and worldly. The desire of the flesh encompasses those desires centered in man's physical nature and are exercised without regard to God's will (Romans 8:3, 8).

THE LUST: DESIRE OF THE EYES

Achan coveted wealth through his eyes (Joshua 7:21). David lusted after Bathsheba, another man's wife through his eyes (2 Samuel 11). Jesus warned about the desire of our eyes: "The eye is the lamp of the body. So, if your eye is healthy, your whole body will be full of light, but if your eye is bad, your whole body will be full of darkness. If then the light in you is darkness, how great is the darkness" (Matthew 6:22-23). Allowing good and right things into our sight will aid us in being the people God desires:

> I will not set before my eyes anything that is worthless. I hate the work of those who fall away; it shall not cling to me. A perverse heart shall be far from me; I will know nothing of evil. Whoever slanders his neighbor secretly I will destroy. Whoever has a haughty look and an arrogant heart I will not endure.
> Psalm 101:3-5

THE PRIDE: VAINGLORY OF LIFE

The sinful use of pride is the exaggerated sense of one's own value or an overly high opinion of oneself. Pride involves the idea of self-sufficiency and denies God a place in our hearts.

The insightful C.S. Lewis stated: "There is no fault which makes a man more unpopular, and no fault which we are more unconscious of in ourselves. And the more we have it ourselves, the more we dislike it in others. The vice I am talking of is Pride or Self-Conceit: and the virtue opposite to it, in Christian morals, is called Humility."[7]

Pride destroys a proper view of self (Proverbs 29:23), a proper view of others (Philippians 2:5-8), and destroys respect for Christ and His Word (1 Timothy 6:3-5).

APPLYING THE PRINCIPLES

"For the grace of God has appeared, bringing salvation for all people, training us to renounce ungodliness and worldly passions, and to live self-controlled, upright, and godly lives in the present age" (Titus 2:11-12). God's grace teaches us to say "no" to ungodliness and worldly lusts. Saying "no" to immoral living will spare us from much pain and suffering. Immoral living damages one's ability to keep the family strong (1 Samuel 2:12; 3:13). It damages one's ability to influence others (Revelation 3:14-17), as well as one's ability to help others (Isaiah 28:7-8). Ungodly lifestyles damage one physically, emotionally, economically, and spiritually.

God's grace also teaches us to say, "yes" to living self-controlled, upright and godly lives. These adverbs describe a trio of focus. First, inward, 'self-controlled,' living is required of the disciple of Christ. Second, outward, 'upright,' directs us to live up to faithfulness in all our actions with others. Third, upward, 'godly,' reminds us to be reverent to God and faithful in our obedience to His Will.

We need direction in deciding whether something is morally right as we navigate through the week between Sundays. The Bible is our standard and having an objective standard avoids chaos.

The Bible speaks to the moral issues of every generation. God's Word is always relevant and can be applied to whatever 'issue' that is current to our society. When facing a dilemma, use the following questions to help determine the proper response.

1. Am I fully persuaded that it is right? (Romans 14:5, 14, 23)

---

7. C.S. Lewis, *Mere Christianity* (San Francisco: HarperOne, 2000), 121.

2. Can I do it as unto the Lord? (Romans 14:6-8)
3. Can I do it without being a stumbling block to my brother or sister in Christ? (Romans 14:13, 15, 20-21)
4. Does it bring peace? (Romans 14:17-18)
5. Does it edify my brother? (Romans 14:19)
6. Is it profitable? (1 Corinthians 6:12)
7. Does it enslave me? (Romans 6:16-18)
8. Does it bring glory to God? (1 Corinthians 10:31)[8]

We hear "do anything you want, anytime you want, anywhere you want." The Bible instructs us to walk as Christ walked, talk as He talked, and live as He lived. When we fail to do so, our soul is endangered. The faithful follower of God is to live in accordance with the principles, beliefs, and practices of the Bible at all times, including between Sundays. To the Philippians, Paul wrote, "Only let your manner of life be worthy of the gospel of Christ, so that whether I come and see you or am absent, I may hear of you that you are standing firm in one spirit, with one mind striving side by side for the faith of the gospel," (Philippians 1:27). The Divine Standard must test all moral questions. While man's thinking may have changed on moral issues, the teachings of God's Word forever remains the same.

---

8. John Feinberg and Paul Feinberg, *Ethics for a Brave New World* (Wheaton: Crossway, 2010), 53-55.

I WILL WALK USING A MORAL COMPASS

QUESTIONS

1. Apply 1 John 2:15-17 to Christian morality.
2. List and describe the three adverbs in Titus 2:11-12.
3. Does the Bible have to say "thou shalt not" for something to be sinful?
4. List an example of the above…as many as you can think of and apply Scripture.
5. What implication exists if one believes there is no absolute moral standard?

9

I WILL WORK HONESTLY

In the current state of our culture, the new norm is to expect something without earning it. This disposition is erroneous and detrimental to us as individuals and to the nation as a whole. Entitlement signals a rejection of the very DNA of Christians. Our God given genetic code is patterned by an honest and ethical view towards working and earning an income that enables us to support ourselves, our families, and to give to those who are in need. Entitlement is a heart problem, a very self-centered one. No one owes us anything! We must work for what we gain.

As Christians, we look to God's Word for direction in our daily lives between Sundays and the Bible has much to say about work.

WORK IN PARADISE

God expects us to work. In the patriarchal age, He charged Adam with dressing and keeping the garden.

> The Lord God took the man and put him in the Garden of Eden to work it and keep it. And the Lord God commanded the man, saying, "You may surely eat of every tree of the garden, but of the tree of the knowledge of good and evil you shall not eat, for in the day that you eat of it you shall surely die." Then the Lord God said, "It is not good that the man should be

alone; I will make him a helper fit for him." Now out of the ground the Lord God had formed every beast of the field and every bird of the heavens and brought them to the man to see what he would call them. And whatever the man called every living creature, that was its name. The man gave names to all livestock and to the birds of the heavens and to every beast of the field.

Genesis 2:15-20

Adam was given the job of naming the animals, which was a responsibility and work.

WORK AFTER THE FALL

From the beginning, the human race was designed for work. Considering the fall, we should not be surprised that work became difficult.

> And to Adam he said, "Because you have listened to the voice of your wife and have eaten of the tree of which I commanded you, 'You shall not eat of it,' cursed is the ground because of you, in pain you shall eat of it all the days of your life; thorns and thistles it shall bring forth for you; and you shall eat the plants of the field. By the sweat of your face you shall eat bread, till you return to the ground, for out of it you were taken; for you are dust, and to dust you shall return."

Genesis 3:17-19

Work is difficult, but it is not a curse.

In the Mosaic age, God charged the Hebrews to labor six days of each week:

> Remember the Sabbath day, to keep it holy. Six days you shall labor, and do all your work, but the seventh day is a Sabbath to the Lord your God. On it you shall not do any work, you, or your son, or your daughter, your male servant, or your female servant, or your livestock, or the sojourner who is within your gates.
>
> Exodus 20:8-10

In the Christian age, it is still God's plan for people to work:

> For that indeed is what you are doing to all the brothers throughout Macedonia. But we urge you, brothers, to do this more and more, and to aspire to live quietly, and to mind your own affairs, and to work with your hands, as we instructed you, so that you may walk properly before outsiders and be dependent on no one.
>
> 1 Thessalonians 4:10-12

Paul issued a warning to those who attempted to bypass the system:

> For you yourselves know how you ought to imitate us, because we were not idle when we were with you, nor did we eat anyone's bread without paying for it, but with toil and labor we worked night and day, that we might not be a burden to any of you. It was not because we do not have that right, but to give you in ourselves an example to imitate. For even when we were with you, we would give you this command: If anyone is not willing to work, let him not eat. For we hear that some among you walk in idleness, not busy at work, but busybodies. Now such persons we command and encourage in the Lord Jesus Christ to do their work quietly and to earn their own living.
>
> 2 Thessalonians 3:7-12

CHRISTIAN WORK ETHIC

Christian work ethics are God-ordained rules, standards and principles governing a worker in his role as an employer or employee. It involves integrity, honesty, commitment, humility, truthfulness, accountability, faithfulness, trustworthiness, positive attitude, behavior, and diligence with the best effort, respect and obedience. Christians that exhibit these qualities in the work place between Sundays allow for a greater influence of Christianity. Living out these mandates is a powerful display of Christ in us.

A SACRED CHARGE

> Bondservants, obey in everything those who are your earthly masters, not by way of eye-service, as people-pleasers, but with sincerity of heart, fearing the Lord. Whatever you do, work heartily, as for the Lord and not for men, knowing that from the Lord you will receive the inheritance as your reward. You are serving the Lord Christ. For the wrongdoer will be paid back for the wrong he has done, and there is no partiality.
>
> Colossians 3:22-25

The working Christian will work "heartily." This is the word for soul, from the depths of your being. Do you realize that when you are working, you are serving God? What does this say about your work productivity (Titus 2:10)? Christians are interested in their faithfulness toward Christ in their work. Therefore, between Sundays, Christians will be the best employees in the world, because they are out of this world thinkers.

> Enjoy life with the wife whom you love, all the days of your vain life that he has given you under the sun, because that is your portion in life and in your toil at which you toil under the sun. Whatever your hand

finds to do, do it with your might, for there is no work or thought or knowledge or wisdom in Sheol, to which you are going.

Ecclesiastes 9:9-10

There are people who accomplish the work; there are procrastinators who rush through with poor quality; there are those who are lazy; there are those who put in the time, but accomplish little; there are the overachievers: those who do more than is necessary for the job and end up with less than desired results because of the pursuit of perfection. There are people that can be depended on to get the job done. Are you one of them?

It is assumed by some managers that employees are inherently lazy and will avoid work if they can, and that they inherently dislike work. There are those who think employees will show little ambition without an enticing incentive program and will avoid responsibility whenever they can. There are also employees who are ambitious and self-motivated and exercise self-control. It is generally conceded by some that employees enjoy their mental and physical work duties. Which is the Biblical model? What should the Christian worker be like between Sundays?

The Christian will do work that is inherently good. Work for what you consume, then work so you can be charitable. Think about what this means as affluence increases. "Let the thief no longer steal, but rather let him labor, doing honest work with his own hands, so that he may have something to share with anyone in need" (Ephesians 4:28).

Employees with a Christian worldview and work ethic are productive. "A slack hand causes poverty, but the hand of the diligent makes rich" (Proverbs 10:4). "In all toil there is profit, but mere talk tends only to poverty" (Proverbs 14:23). In other words, talk is cheap, and some talk their way into being unproductive. There will always be excuses to offer when you do not have the discipline to work: "The sluggard says, "There is a lion outside! I shall be killed in the streets" (Proverbs 22:13)!

BALANCE

In working honestly as a child of God between Sundays, we will be conscious of the importance of maintaining balance between work and time for family and God.

> You and I have an average of about seventy or eighty years on this earth. During these years we are bombarded with the temporary. Make money. Get stuff. Be comfortable. Live well. Have fun. In the middle of it all, we get blinded to the eternal. But it's there. You and I stand on the porch of eternity. Both of us will soon stand before God to give an account for our stewardship of the time, the resources, the gifts, and ultimately the gospel he has entrusted to us. When that day comes, I am convinced we will not wish we had given more of ourselves to living the American dream. We will not wish we had made more money, acquired more stuff, lived more comfortably, taken more vacations, watched more television, pursued greater retirement, or been more successful in the eyes of this world. Instead we will wish we had given more of ourselves to living for the day when every nation, tribe, people, and language will bow around the throne and sing the praises of the Savior who delights in radical obedience and the God who deserves eternal worship.[1]

COMMUNICATION

What do you communicate in the work world between Sundays? The Bible has much to say regarding our presentation to those in the world. "Walk in wisdom toward outsiders, making the best use of the time. Let your speech always be gracious, seasoned with salt,

---

1. David Platt, *Radical* (Colorado Springs: Multnomah, 2010), 216.

so that you may know how you ought to answer each person" (Colossians 3:4-5). "Keep your conduct among the Gentiles honorable, so that when they speak against you as evildoers, they may see your good deeds and glorify God on the day of visitation" (1 Peter 2:12).

CHRISTIAN AS A BUSINESS LEADER

Our lives between Sundays find us interacting and working alongside others in the workforce. Scripture reminds us of our responsibility, no matter our position. "Masters, treat your bondservants justly and fairly, knowing that you also have a Master in heaven" (Colossians 4:1). "The greatest among you shall be your servant. Whoever exalts himself will be humbled, and whoever humbles himself will be exalted" (Matthew 23:11-12). Jesus identified the example His disciples should exhibit in the world, including the workplace. "But Jesus called them to him and said, 'You know that the rulers of the Gentiles lord it over them, and their great ones exercise authority over them. It shall not be so among you. But whoever would be great among you must be your servant'" (Matthew 20:25-26).

Leaders use the term 'we.' They understand that they are part of the team. Every member is a key player (Luke 22:26). Leaders never think of themselves as better than everyone else. They recognize that every human resource is a valuable contributor (Romans 12:3). Leaders care about the people who work in their organization. They know where the organization is headed and have a plan for getting there. True leaders can be trusted. They are fair, and they keep their word. "The righteous who walks in his integrity—blessed are his children after him" (Proverbs 20:7)! Leaders are objective. They are guided by wise decisions and reasoning. "The steps of a man are established by the Lord, when he delights in his way" (Psalm 37:23). Leaders understand the importance of earning respect and having a good reputation, as opposed to focusing only on the bottom line. "A good name is to be chosen rather than great riches, and favor is better than silver or gold" (Proverbs 22:1).

Between Sundays the Christian as manager understands that

the ultimate leader is God, and seeking Him is paramount to success. The Christian is to pray continuously and in all actions. Personal characteristics are to be modeled after the Fruit of the Spirit. "But the fruit of the Spirit is love, joy, peace, patience, kindness, goodness, faithfulness, gentleness, self-control" (Galatians 5:22-23). He/she plans projects with careful consideration. "For which of you, desiring to build a tower, does not first sit down and count the cost, whether he has enough to complete it" (Luke 14:28)? The Christian manager supports the promotion and success of his/her employees. "Let each of you look not only to his own interests, but also to the interests of others" (Philippians 2:4). The manager will seek to communicate vision and goals with clear motivation. "Write the vision; make it plain on tablets, so he may run who reads it" (Habakkuk 2:2). The Christian leader will strive to exhibit excellence and diligence in the work place. "Do you see a man skillful in his work? He will stand before kings; he will not stand before obscure men" (Proverbs 22:29).

AREAS OF CONCERN

The Christian in the workplace faces many challenges and temptations. There will be pressures to conform to the company's culture, and the Christian will be faced with decisions that will impact their influence and character. These are concerns that generally occur between Sundays.

Here are five common areas of concern in the workplace:

TONGUE

The tongue speaks from the heart of the individual. "But what comes out of the mouth proceeds from the heart, and this defiles a person. For out of the heart come evil thoughts, murder, adultery, sexual immorality, theft, false witness, slander. These are what defile a person" (Matthew 15:18-20). What do we reveal to our co-workers? Are we known for a 'sharp' tongue, or are we known for speech that is kind and considerate and objective?

Communication in the workplace should be viewed as an opportunity for the Christian to build a reputation for being respectable, relationship building, and professional. The tongue is powerful, and it can undo in moments what took years to accomplish and build.

> How great a forest is set ablaze by such a small fire! And the tongue is a fire, a world of unrighteousness. The tongue is set among our members, staining the whole body, setting on fire the entire course of life, and set on fire by hell. For every kind of beast and bird, of reptile and sea creature, can be tamed and has been tamed by mankind, but no human being can tame the tongue. It is a restless evil, full of deadly poison. With it we bless our Lord and Father, and with it we curse people who are made in the likeness of God. From the same mouth come blessing and cursing. My brothers, these things ought not to be so.
>
> James 3:5-10

HONESTY

Have you lied for your boss? Is there a co-worker who has witnessed you telling a little 'white lie'? Do your employees think lying is acceptable under your leadership? It is believed that Americans lie often. Exaggerations, embellishments, deceit, misleading others, fraud, cheating, and misinformation are often in contrast to and in favor of accuracy, facts, and truth telling. What happened to integrity (true to one's word), credibility (pattern of believability), and faithfulness (do what you say you will do…keep your promises in our own words and actions)? "Whoever speaks the truth gives honest evidence, but a false witness utters deceit" (Proverbs 12:17). "Lying lips are an abomination to the Lord, but those who act faithfully are his delight" (Proverbs 12:22). Consistency demands we cannot be honest at home and dishonest at work. "Pray for us, for we are sure that we have a clear conscience, desiring to act honorably in all things" (Hebrews 13:18).

ALCOHOL

> Who has woe? Who has sorrow?
>   Who has strife? Who has complaining?
> Who has wounds without cause?
>   Who has redness of eyes?
> Those who tarry long over wine;
>   those who go to try mixed wine.
> Do not look at wine when it is red,
>   when it sparkles in the cup
>   and goes down smoothly.
> In the end it bites like a serpent
>   and stings like an adder.
> Your eyes will see strange things,
>   and your heart utter perverse things.
> You will be like one who lies down in the midst of the sea,
>   like one who lies on the top of a mast.
> "They struck me," you will say, "but I was not hurt;
>   they beat me, but I did not feel it.
> When shall I awake?
>   I must have another drink."
>
> Proverbs 23:29-35

The office staff is going to the club for drinks after work. "You are coming right? As Christians, we are to "abstain from every form of evil" (1Thessalonians 5:22). Peter stated: "With respect to this they are surprised when you do not join them in the same flood of debauchery, and they malign you" (1 Peter 4:4).

There are no positive benefits of a Christian drinking alcoholic beverages socially. The Christian is to always "be sober-minded; be watchful. Your adversary the devil prowls around like a roaring lion, seeking someone to devour" (1 Peter 5:8). The individual consuming alcohol is more likely to speak insultingly to others. They are prone to become violent and argumentative. The increased mindset to commit sexual sins and participate in other vices, including impairment to our decision making and being wasteful with money, is accelerated by alcoholic beverages. The family name and reputation are also at stake when one drinks alcohol.

Are we being the influence Jesus would have us to be by consuming alcoholic beverages? When others see us drinking alcoholic beverages, we damage our influence, and God is not honored. Once we have destroyed our influence; it is extremely difficult to teach the truth (1 Timothy 4:12-16).

GREED

We are sometimes tempted with a desire for more than is needed, especially in material things. Men and women can engage in work for the wrong reasons. Being greedy for more is far too often the temptation of the world in which we live. "A rich man's wealth is his strong city, and like a high wall in his imagination" (Proverbs 18:11). Money can be a powerful influence upon an individual. The wrong view of wealth can lead to covetousness.

> As a form of idolatry (Col. 3:5), the love of "goods" cancels out faith in God, since no one can have two absolute masters (Luke 16:13). Greed can create the anxiety, depression, and loss of meaning that often comes in middle age after "successful" life of acquiring the "goods" of this world. Greed tempts us to other forms of corruption, such as lying, swindling, cheating clients, and cheating the government.[2]

Covetousness is a detrimental desire. It hinders generosity and

---

2. Robert C. Roberts, "Just a Little Bit More: Greed and the Malling of Our Souls," *Moral Issues and Christian Responses*, edited by Patricia Beattie Jung, and L. Shannon Jung (Minneapolis: Fortress Press), 292.

is often the motive for offenses against one's neighbor and is self-destructive.

PRIDE

God teaches us the cure for sinful pride is found in at least two qualities: (1) love: "Love is patient and kind; love does not envy or boast; it is not arrogant" (1 Corinthians 13:4), and (2) humility: "Do nothing from selfish ambition or conceit, but in humility count others more significant than yourselves" (Philippians 2:3).

Do you have pride under control in your work life? Are you quick to find fault with others and to express those thoughts to others? Are you gratified of the schedule you keep, how disciplined you are, how much you can accomplish? Are you motivated to receive approval, praise, or acceptance from others? Do you generally consider your way is the right way, the only way, or the best way? Do you have a quick-tempered, sensitive spirit? Are you easily offended?

All these areas of concern affect our example to others and can have a negative impact as we seek to lead effectively in the workplace between Sundays and live out our Christian example.

Working renders a service to others and brings personal growth and development. Whatever our work schedule between Sundays, we are to be consistent in living as a Christian. We must be careful and avoid the temptation to compartmentalize our work life from our Christian life. Work provides the necessities of life. Honest labor prevents the temptation of idleness.

All days, including between Sundays, remember: "In all your ways acknowledge him, and he will make straight your paths" (Proverbs 3:6). "So, whether you eat or drink, or whatever you do, do all to the glory of God" (1 Corinthians 10:31). Christianity is not something we put on the first day of the week, like our Sunday apparel, and take off when we get home.

QUESTIONS

1. What are some characteristics of the Christian work ethic?
2. Who do we ultimately work for?
3. Apply Ephesians 4:28 to our work life.
4. List some features of the Christian business leader.
5. Discuss God's command for man to work in the patriarchal, mosaic, and Christian age.

10

I WILL BALANCE MY RESPONSIBILITIES

In 1 Kings 20, Ben-hadad, King of Syria, tried to strong-arm Israel by demanding whatever he wanted (2-6). He relayed that he would turn Samaria into dust and was disregarded by Ahab. Ben-hadad and the thirty-two kings who were with him were drinking and were not successful in battle against Israel because a prophet had told Ahab God would give the Syrians over to them. God warned Ahab that he would attempt to attack Israel again the next spring. Ben-hadad was persuaded that he lost because of the location of the battle, so he decided to attack thereafter on a plain. God again channels Ahab into a huge victory. Ben-hadad resolves that it would be noble to plead for mercy. Ben-hadad offers terms of peace and Ahab permits Ben-hadad to be set free (20:23-34). This was against God's will in the matter since he wanted Ben-hadad destroyed (20:42). God sent a prophet to Ahab with an illustration. The man disguises himself as a wounded soldier (20:37-38). He conveys to the king that he was entrusted to guard a soldier with his life and if the soldier escaped, it would be his life for the escaped solider as well as paying a talent of silver (20:39-40). The excuse: **"And as your servant was busy here and there, he was gone"** (20:40; emphasis mine). This was to show Ahab's neglect in following God's orders.

The last of the passage reveals the "rest of the story." "Then he hurried to take the bandage away from his eyes, and the king of Israel recognized him as one of the prophets. And he said to him, 'Thus says the Lord, 'Because you have let go out of your hand the man whom I had devoted to destruction, therefore your life shall be for his life, and your people for his people." And the king of Israel went to his house vexed and sullen and came to Samaria" (20:41-43). Ahab allowed Ben-hadad, the prisoner, to escape. God had condemned Ben-hadad to ruin, and Ahab set him free to create political and economic gain for himself. Ahab announced his own judgment, and with his life he would pay for the life of Ben-hadad whom he let go. Distraction and being 'too busy' was disastrous for Ahab and reminds us that our being overly busy is not always a mark of advantage.

BUSY HERE & THERE

We must admit it. We are like Ahab. Between Sundays, we are sometimes too busy to accomplish our purpose in this life. The world programs us to think busy means productive. The result is our Christian walk with God tragically suffers. One writer has lamented: "Somewhere around the end of the 20th century, busyness became not just a way of life but a badge of honor. And life, sociologists say, became an exhausting everydayathon."[1]

REASONS FOR OUR BUSYNESS

There are at least two reasons we are busy here and there and fail to accomplish our God-given mission in this life:

- **Faithlessness.** We do not trust God to accomplish things in our absence, without our involvement. So, we over schedule our time, our family's time, our work time, our recreation time and our God-time. "We disappoint God and his priorities in our lives rather than the men and women around us." We live a life of stress.

---

1. Brigid Shulte, https://www.washingtonpost.com/opinions/why-being-too-busy-makes-us-feel-so-good/2014/03/14/c098f6c8-9e81-11e3-a050-dc3322a94fa7_story.html.

Our physical body is neglected, and we lack sleep, proper diet, and exercise. The worst part of all is that we become spiritually crippled by our busyness.

- **Foolishness.** The idea that believing our busyness makes us important. As one writer stated it: Busyness does not mean I am diligent. Busyness does not mean I am *faithful*. Busyness does not mean I am fruitful. [2]

"People compete over being busy; it's about showing status." If you're busy, you're important. You're leading a full and worthy life…Keeping up with the Joneses used to be about money, cars and homes. Now, she explains, "If you're not as busy as the Joneses, you'd better get cracking."[3]

REPLICAS OF OUR BUSYNESS

My **Family** *Was Gone*

In a survey of the Top 10 Issues Facing Today's Family by Lifeway Research, "busyness" was listed #3, right after Anti-Christian culture and divorce.[4] Successful, godly families are united families. Our busyness today is hindering our togetherness as a family. Many families are divided into separate activities with everyone going in different directions; failing to enjoy one another's support and company in everyday life. Extra educational functions, church activities, the arts, community involvement, and sports are consuming families and their time both individually and collectively.

Does it ever cross anyone's mind today that there is value in spending time together as a family unit? Eating meals together? Going on trips and outings, sharing life with each other? Some families

---

2. C.J. Mahaney, Biblical Productivity, 2009 Sovereign Grace Ministries. www.SovereignGraceMinistries.org.

3. Brigid Shulte.

4. http://www.biblicalfoundations.org/the-top-10-issues-facing-marriage-and-family-today-an-assessment/.

are so divided that one parent goes one direction with one or two and the spouse goes in the opposite direction with one or two or more; all because of over commitment. There is value in extra activities which are educational, recreational, and that stimulate and enable growth. However, Satan is successful in feeding us the lie that staying busy 24/7 somehow makes us smart and important.

What example are we setting as parents when we allow the world to dictate our schedule between Sundays? What influence are we having on our children when ball practice or another activity is chosen instead of Wednesday night Bible study? Do we expect our children to view our choice for them in any other context; except, "church" is not as important as your extra activities? Why the shock over losing our young people when they go off to college? We have simply set the example before them stating God, Christ and the church are second to everything else.

My **Church** *Was Gone*

Being a member of the body of Christ, the church, is a great privilege because it is meant to be a place of safety, fellowship, love, and forgiveness. It is essential we contribute to the church our complete devotion and service. Edification (building up one another) is one of the many benefits we receive. "Rather, speaking the truth in love, we are to grow up in every way into him who is the head, into Christ, from whom the whole body, joined and held together by every joint with which it is equipped, when each part is working properly, makes the body grow so that it builds itself up in love" (Ephesians 4:15-16).

Encouragement is to be given to one another in the body. "And let us consider how to stir up one another to love and good works" (Hebrews 10:24). Teaching and admonishing helps us grow, develop, and mature as Christians. "Let the word of Christ dwell in you richly, teaching and admonishing one another in all wisdom, singing psalms and hymns and spiritual songs, with thankfulness in your hearts to God" (Colossians 3:16). We must bear our burdens with one another as we live out each day in this world of trouble and despair. "Bear one another's burdens, and so fulfill the law of Christ" (Galatians 6:2). The apostle Paul encouraged the Thessalonians to help one another when death affects our brothers and sisters. "Therefore encourage one another with these words" (1 Thessalonians 4:18). To forgive in the spirit of Christ is necessary in our relationship to each other and to our Savior. "Be kind to one another, tenderhearted, forgiving one another, as God in Christ forgave you" (Ephesians 4:32).

Working together, serving, worshipping, and helping in the name of Christ maintains and expands the kingdom of God by allowing Christ to work through us in doing His will. "Only let your manner of life be worthy of the gospel of Christ, so that whether I come and see you or am absent, I may hear of you that you are standing firm in one spirit, with one mind striving side by side for the faith of the gospel" (Philippians 1:27).

Distractions. The technology and communication avenues of our age have changed personal interaction. We are programed to use applications (apps) that often take the place of personal interaction. As Christians, we must always be reminded that "church" is not an app; it is who we are. Let us use technology to offer encouragement; but not lose the value of physical touch, conversation and expression. There is no app for shaking someone's hand. There is no app for bearing the burden of a struggling brother or sister in Christ. There is no app for hugging a church member who has not been there in weeks. There is no app for telling a young person how proud you are of them. There is no app to encourage the widow who struggles to attend service because of her health. Church…there is no app for that. It is a lifestyle, a choice and a hope!

The challenge to stay balanced in a world that is physical while at the same time "online," is acknowledged when we think of the advantages and disadvantages of technology and the distractions that occur.

The advances of technology via the Internet and social media have provided many avenues for Christians to share their faith and interact with others in presenting our unique worldview. Communication has increased because we can within seconds contact a brother or sister in Christ. Our congregations have opportunities to share events, teaching points, sermons, and helpful comments on our culture or world events. Information from the Bible can be shared and taught, edifying, and encouraging people around the world. Our community in Christ has increased opportunities to influence others for Christ. Think of how visitors can learn about us without ever stepping into one of our services. Technology has magnified the preaching of the gospel; we can have a worldwide audience. Many more advantages exist and as technology continues to evolve, the uses could be endless in the advancement of the Christian faith.

One of the major disadvantages in the realm of technology is the distraction and harm that can come to our relationships in the home and in the church. Hours can disappear from our schedules daily by spending too much time in the virtual world of the Internet. Responsibilities to our spouse, children, brothers and sisters in Christ, our job, and not to mention our neighbors and friends, fail to get accomplished because of our being distracted by technology.

Being "busy here and there" can be detrimental to our work in every area if we are not careful and vigilant.

When we value something, we give it our best. How much do we value the church?

My Opportunity *Was Gone*

> Now as they went on their way, Jesus entered a village. And a woman named Martha welcomed him into her house. And she had a sister called Mary, who sat at the Lord's feet and listened to his teaching. But Martha was distracted with much serving. And she went up to him and said, "Lord, do you not care that my sister has left me to serve alone? Tell her then to help me." But the Lord answered her, "Martha, Martha, you are anxious and troubled about many things, but one thing is necessary. Mary has chosen the good portion, which will not be taken away from her."
>
> Luke 10:38-42

Self-Centeredness. Jesus was in their house. The most honored guest in our homes is Jesus Christ. Martha was distracted with 'much serving.' Mary sat at the feet of Jesus and listened intently to His teaching. The song "What would you do if Jesus came to spend some time with you" comes to mind in this story. Our opportunities in life may be squandered through self-centeredness. "But Martha was distracted with much serving. And she went up to him and said, 'Lord, do you not care that my sister has left me to serve alone? Tell her then to help me'" (Luke 10:40). We must be careful that even if we are doing a good thing, there may be something more important that needs our attention and will be of benefit to us and others.

Separation from God. We cannot afford to have disorganized priorities when it comes to acknowledging God and His Son. Our lack of keeping first things first will cost us. We should say with the Psalmist: "One thing have I asked of the Lord, that will I seek after: that I may dwell in the house of the Lord all the days of my life, to gaze upon the beauty of the Lord and to inquire in his temple. For he will hide me in his shelter in the day of trouble; he will conceal me under the cover of his tent; he will lift me high upon a rock" (Psalm 27:4-5).

Sacrifice of "Better Things." Mary chose the "good portion" which Jesus said would not be taken away from her.

Martha allowed herself to become distracted doing a good work when she could have been sitting at the feet of Jesus. She would later show her commitment to the Lord at the death of Lazarus (John 11:17-29). With costly ointment, Mary later anoints Jesus for burial (John 12:1-8).

How many times are we distracted in life when the here and now obstructs our view of eternity? One writer observes: "It requires strong and steady resolve to live out the gospel in the middle of an American dream that identifies success as moving up the ladder, getting the bigger house, purchasing the nicer car, buying the better clothes, eating the finer food, and acquiring more things."[5]

---

5. David Platt, *Radical* (Colorado Springs: Multnomah, 2010),136.

My **Soul** *Was Gone*

As the song reminds us: "Brother afar from the Savior today, risking your soul for the things that decay. Oh if today, God should call you away, what would you give in exchange for your soul?" "For what will it profit a man if he gains the whole world and forfeits his soul? Or what shall a man give in return for his soul" (Matthew 16:26)?

Busyness consumes us here on earth and can easily distract us from our ultimate goal: Heaven! The most valuable possession any human being has is his soul. If we are too busy to care, feed, and direct our own soul in the ways of God, then we are setting ourselves up for failure in regard to taking possession of our eternal home with God. Our Lord knew we would have the choice to trade our soul away.

What will you trade your most precious commodity for? Power? Prestige? Pleasure? Possessions? We should follow the example of Christ and seek balance in our everyday activities where God and His kingdom are first and everything else falls in behind (1 Peter 5:6-7).

THE REVERSAL OF OUR BUSYNESS

Let us finally consider how we can reverse the devastating trend many of us have found ourselves trapped in regarding day and time. We must restore quality to our schedules between Sundays.

We must make sure we include God in all our plans by establishing Biblical priorities in our lives. It is prudent to make time for God all through the week.

> Come now, you who say, "Today or tomorrow we will go into such and such a town and spend a year there and trade and make a profit"— yet you do not know what tomorrow will bring. What is your life? For you are a mist that appears for a little time and then vanishes. Instead you ought to say, "If the Lord wills, we

will live and do this or that." As it is, you boast in your arrogance. All such boasting is evil. So whoever knows the right thing to do and fails to do it, for him it is sin.

James 4:13-17

Set Goals

Setting goals between Sundays can clarify our purposes and responsibilities. Keeping realistic goals in focus can help us in the areas of accountability and will motivate us in accomplishing our directives. Remember, "There are many plans in a man's heart, nevertheless the Lord's counsel—that will stand" (Proverbs 19:2).

Eliminate Excuses

We must be honest with ourselves and be straightforward with others regarding what we are willing and able to do.

> As they were going along the road, someone said to him, "I will follow you wherever you go." And Jesus said to him, "Foxes have holes, and birds of the air have nests, but the Son of Man has nowhere to lay his head." To another he said, "Follow me." But he said, "Lord, let me first go and bury my father." And Jesus said to him, "Leave the dead to bury their own dead. But as for you, go and proclaim the kingdom of God." Yet another said, "I will follow you, Lord, but let me first say farewell to those at my home." Jesus said to him, "No one who puts his hand to the plow and looks back is fit for the kingdom of God."

Luke 9:57-62

Redeem the Time

"Look carefully then how you walk, not as unwise but as wise, making the best use of the time, because the days are evil" (Ephesians 5:15-16).

How do we find time to be still between Sundays? We must schedule that time. We all know if anything is to be accomplished in our lives it is because we schedule it, right? We schedule our work, exercise, recreation, and our entertainment. However, first and foremost, we must schedule time with God! Sometimes we just need to take the time to, "Be still and know that I am God" (Psalm 46:10).

QUESTIONS

1. How does Ahab's neglect in 1 Kings 20 relate to being too busy?
2. In Luke 10:38-42, what does Jesus say about Mary and her choice?
3. The example of Martha in being distracted has implications for us today. Discuss.
4. How can we reverse our busyness?
5. How can we use technology in such a way that it will not distract us?

11

I WILL PRAY WITHOUT CEASING

Between Sundays, we must pray. A man who studied deeply about prayer, Edward McKendree Bounds, wrote: "We do more of everything else than of praying." In being honest with ourselves, we are just like the disciples who said: "Lord, teach us to pray" (Luke 11:1). "I need help and instruction in my prayer life;" or "I don't know what to say" are probably two of the most common statements from our lips when we are discussing the subject of prayer. We reason; "why pray if God already knows my needs" (Matthew 6:8)? "I am not revealing anything He does not already know." James gives us insight into the fact there are some things God will not grant us until we ask: "You desire and do not have…You do not have, because you do not ask" (James 4:2).

Prayer helps the Christian in the areas of dependence on God and our thankfulness to Him for all He has done and continues to do in our lives. A faithful, consistent prayer life brings us into a deeper, personal, fellowship with God our Father.

Paul wrote to the Colossians; "Devote yourselves to prayer, with an alert mind and a thankful heart" (Colossians 4:2 NLT). The apostles are on record as saying: "But we will devote ourselves to prayer and to the ministry of the word" (Acts 6:4). How devoted are you to faithful, consistent prayer to God the Father?

Prayer is real. It is an intentional, authentic avenue of communication with Deity. Prayer is conversation, the intercourse of the soul with God. Christian prayer has been defined as "an offering up of our desires unto God, for things agreeable to his will, in the name of Christ, with confession of our sins, and thankful acknowledgment of his mercies,"[1] as well as "a correspondence fixed with heaven."[2]

THE ATTRIBUTES OF GOD

A study of God's characteristics can help us in our prayer lives. In order to communicate with our Heavenly Father, we must know Him and seek to understand His ways and His interest in every aspect of our daily lives. J. I. Packer has acknowledged: "What were we made for? To know God. What aim should we set ourselves in life? To know God."[3] Knowing more about God will fill our souls with His love, mercy, and grace and teach us to better understand what to ask for and how to properly receive His answers, all in the context of living between Sundays.

A deep love and respect for God will be evident in the content of our prayers and in the depths of our soul. "I will give thanks to the Lord with my whole heart; I will recount all of your wonderful deeds. I will be glad and exult in you; I will sing praise to your name, O Most High" (Psalm 9:1-2). God is great, all good, all-powerful and all knowing. We worship God for being the unchanging faithful God that He has evidenced in His Word.

God has incommunicable (characteristics belonging only to God) attributes that we should study and honor with thanksgiving, godly fear, and reverence.

Unlimited in His Existence. God revealed Himself as "I AM" in Genesis 3:14. "For as the Father has life in himself, so he has granted the Son also to have life in himself" (John. 5:26). God's self-sufficiency is emphasized throughout Scripture: "Who has first given to me, that I should repay him? Whatever is under the whole heaven is mine" (Job 41:11).

---

1. *Westminster Shorter Catechism.*

2. Robert Burns, as quoted in Herbert Lockyer *All The Prayers Of The Bible* (Grand Rapids: Zondervan, 1959), 18.

3. J. I. Packer, *Knowing God* (Downers Grove, IL: Inter-Varsity, 1993), 33.

Unlimited in Regard to Time. God is without beginning or end: "Before the mountains were brought forth, or ever you had formed the earth and the world, from everlasting to everlasting you are God" (Psalm. 90:2). "Of old you laid the foundation of the earth, and the heavens are the work of your hands. They will perish, but you will remain; they will all wear out like a garment. You will change them like a robe, and they will pass away, but you are the same, and your years have no end" (Psalm 102:25-27). Our existence here on the earth is directed by time (years, months, days, weeks, hours, minutes), but God is not restricted since He has always existed and is outside the sphere of time: "I am the Lord; that is my name; my glory I give to no other, nor my praise to carved idols. Behold, the former things have come to pass, and new things I now declare; before they spring forth I tell you of them" (Isaiah 42:8-9).

Unlimited in Regard to Space. Space limits us. We can only be in one place at a time. These limitations do not exist for God. "Am I a God at hand, declares the Lord, and not a God far away? Can a man hide himself in secret places so that I cannot see him? declares the Lord. Do I not fill heaven and earth? declares the Lord" (Jeremiah 23:23-24).

ATTRIBUTES OF INTELLECT: OMNISCIENCE

Unlimited in His Knowledge. Our God is perfect in knowledge (Job 37:16) and "knows everything" (1 John 3:20). That God is not limited by space or time demands this conclusion. "And no creature is hidden from his sight, but all are naked and exposed to the eyes of him to whom we must give account" (Hebrews 4:13). God knows all things actual and potential (Matthew 11:21). God is all-wise. God acts upon His knowledge to always do what is infinitely best. "Oh, the depth of the riches and wisdom and knowledge of God! How unsearchable are his judgments and how inscrutable his ways! 'For who has known the mind of the Lord, or who has been his counselor?' 'Or who has given a gift to him that he might be repaid?' For from him and through him and to him are all things. To him be glory forever.

Amen" (Romans 11:33-36).

ATTRIBUTES OF WILL: OMNIPOTENCE

Unlimited in His Power. It was Job who said, "I know that you can do all things, and that no purpose of yours can be thwarted" (Job 42:2). God is able to do anything He wills. He will not do anything against His nature (sin) or anything that is logically self-contradictory. God is all-powerful. He is not limited in what He wills to accomplish. "Ah, Lord God! It is you who have made the heavens and the earth by your great power and by your outstretched arm! Nothing is too hard for you...The word of the Lord came to Jeremiah: 'Behold, I am the Lord, the God of all flesh. Is anything too hard for me'" (Jeremiah 32:17, 27)? God cannot do or will to do anything that would violate His character or compromise any of His attributes. God cannot lie (Titus 1:2). He cannot cease to exist. God is the final authority, He is sovereign (1 Chronicles 29:11,12), the ruler over all the affairs of the universe.

GOD IS INTERESTED IN US

God is love and is incomprehensibly active for our good will (1 John 4:8). He owns the attribute of grace (unmerited favor), which gives us salvation (Ephesians 2:8). He is a God that is merciful, full of concern and compassion (James 5:11). Our God is just. God is perfectly righteous and exact in His dealings with man (Psalm 19:9).

We all have needs and concerns in our lives, and God is totally interested in our well-being. Petitioning God, as a Father, who cares for us will be a daily practice. "Therefore I tell you, whatever you ask in prayer, believe that you have received it, and it will be yours" (Mark 11:24). He desires our petitions in faith, sincerity and selflessness. Pray honestly and with specificity. God knows what is in our heart and we must be honest to share our petitions, struggles, fears, obstacles, and concerns, seeking His counsel and help in our lives.

It is imperative that we pray continually between Sundays. The deeper we know God and His qualities, the more beneficial and praiseworthy our prayers will be. It is important to remember God answers prayer by saying yes (Jonah 1:1-2:10), no (2 Corinthians 12:7-10), delayed (Job 30:20; Acts 12:1-17), and modifications to our requests (John 11:1-44).

As we pray in faith, remember not to forsake God as we wait for an answer. Remember our prayers simply may be delayed. Remember our prayers must be in accordance with God's will. Remember God's perspective: "'For My thoughts are not your thoughts, nor are your ways My ways,' says the Lord. 'For as the heavens are higher than the earth, so are My ways higher than your ways, and My thoughts than your thoughts'" (Isaiah 55:8-9).

JESUS, PRAYER, AND GOD'S WILL

Jesus prayed about God's will: "Thy will be done on earth as it is in heaven" (Matthew 6:10). Jesus subjected His will to the Father's (John 17:4). Prayers are often only concerned with our own will, while ignoring God's will for our lives. James rebukes this attitude in us: "You ought to say, if the Lord wills we will live and also do this or that" (James 4:15). The Lord wants us to be concerned with His will being accomplished in our hearts, in our lives, and in the lives of others. Whether small or large in their intensity, we should seek God's will to take precedence with every prayer.

Jesus led a powerful prayer life and encouraged the same of His disciples (John 15:7). Jesus demonstrated faith and obedience through prayer (Matthew 21:22; 7:7-11), and also spent quiet time in prayer (Matthew 14:23). Jesus prayed with others (Mark 9:2), before partaking of daily blessings (Mark 6:41), and He prayed for His disciples (John 17).

DECISIONS

Why is praying before a decision important to us? Prayer keeps us in tune with God's will and God's purpose. To know God's will and God's purpose, we must know God. And the only way to know God is to spend time with God in prayer and in His Word. How does this apply to us? It is easy to go through life making all sorts of decisions without considering what God may want in each of those circumstances.

Praying before important decisions reorients us toward God. It causes us to ask:

- What does God want for me?
- What is His mind and wisdom about this opportunity?
- Why have I been placed in this circumstance?
- What lessons have I learned from past decisions?

God's Word reminds us that God is in charge. We reverence our Creator by living our lives allowing our plans to be directed by His.

THE EXAMPLE OF THE EARLY CHURCH

We have a great cloud of witnesses who passed into eternity having served God on earth. Their example gives us great insight into how the church utilized prayer in their daily lives. They continued with one accord in prayer and supplication" (Acts 1:14-24). They "continued steadfastly…" (Acts 2:24). The Apostles gave themselves "continually to prayer" (Acts 6:6). Peter prayed…Cornelius sent for him (Acts 10:9). The early Christians prayed for Peter without ceasing (Acts 12:5). We find that they prayed on many different occasions: "About midnight Paul and Silas were praying and singing hymns to God, and the prisoners were listening to them" (Acts 16:25). The early church believed in and practiced prayer because they knew God and relied on Him and His Will for their lives.

PRAY FOR

What do you pray for between Sundays? Are you ever hindered

in your prayers trying to decide what to pray? The following is only the beginning of categories in which we can find numerous examples to include in our prayers to God.

- Self
- Family
- Community
- Church
- Nation
- Non-Believers
- The Sick
- The Poor and Oppressed

Several of these relate to interceding on others' behalf. "First of all, then, I urge that supplications, prayers, intercessions, and thanksgivings be made for all people, for kings and all who are in high positions, that we may lead a peaceful and quiet life, godly and dignified in every way" (1 Timothy 2:1-2). Praying for others (all people; even enemies) is an integral part of our Christian lifestyle between Sundays.

PRAY MORE

We need to learn to pray more. "It is, therefore, a most benevolent and gracious provision of the Scheme of Redemption that God permits, invites, and encourages his children to pray; to pray always, to pray every-where, and to pray for all things that are necessary to their present and eternal well-being"[4] Most Christians would admit they could pray more. The distractions of the world and our busy daily lives often crowd out prayer. We cannot wait until we "need" God or pray only when something happens that we cannot handle.

---

4. Robert Milligan, *The Scheme Of Redemption* (Nashville: Gospel Advocate Company,1975), 367.

We need to communicate and depend on God at all times; positive and negative, trusting that He knows best and will assist in our lives.

Prayer is real and involves talking to God. God is everywhere all the time and has the power and goodness to answer our prayers, knowing what we need better than we do.

Do we realize how much time we are blessed with between Sundays and how we need to utilize much of it in prayer?

> Prayer is, of course, more than mere thinking, but thinking God's thoughts as he has revealed them is the basis for addressing God in prayer. Having revealed his purpose God allows us to be involved in the carrying out of his will as his dear children. He gives us the privilege of identifying with his will by asking him to do it. This is part of the process he has chosen to use in order to carry out his plan for the whole universe. If we are to ask for anything "according to his will" (1 John 5:14), then we must refer to his will as revealed in his word. Faith in prayer is not what we dream up but is engendered by hearing the word of Christ (Rom 10:17).[5]

May our prayers give God the glory as well as the answers to prayer that God delivers. Among those great cloud of witnesses, are those who utilized prayer and: "who through faith conquered kingdoms, enforced justice, obtained promises, stopped the mouths of lions, quenched the power of fire, escaped the edge of the sword, were made strong out of weakness, became mighty in war, put foreign armies to flight" (Hebrews 11:33-34).

Take an inventory of your daily prayer life. Be a person of prayer between Sundays.

---

5. Graeme Goldsworthy, "A Biblical-Theological Perspective on Prayer," *Prayer and the Knowledge of God* (Downers Grove, IL: InterVarsity, 2003).

QUESTIONS

1. In your own words, define prayer.
2. Discuss the example of the early church and their example of prayer.
3. List two attributes of God and relate those to our prayer life and how we view God.
4. What are some questions we should ask when praying about important decisions?
5. What possible answers does God give us to our prayers?

12

I WILL FULFILL MY ROLE IN THE HOME

Under the heading, "Who Needs Marriage?" a Time Magazine study concluded: "What we found is that marriage, whatever its social, spiritual, or symbolic appeal, is in purely practical terms just not as necessary as it used to be."[1] This observation is a reflection of where we are in recent times when it comes to the subject of marriage and the family. As we engage others in our days between Sundays, we are confronted with other worldviews of marriage.

Christians believe the family is a necessary component of any society and will be present in any successful environment. Albert Mohler has well stated:

> We believe that humanity needs marriage. God created the institution of marriage — defined on his terms — as the central institution of human society. Marriage was given to us by our Creator as the central institution for sexual relatedness, procreation, and the nurture of children. But, even beyond these goods, God gave us marriage as an institution central to human happiness and flourishing. Rightly understood, marriage is essential even to the happiness and flourishing of the unmarried. It is just that central to

---

1. Time Magazine, Nov. 18, 2010. http://content.time.com/time/magazine/article/0,9171,2032116,00.html.

human existence, and not by accident.[2]

GOD DESIGNED ORIGIN

The Scriptures are our only source of information about the origin of marriage. Jesus said, "Have you not read…" (Matthew 19:4), in the context of marriage. God created male and female and provided the marriage relationship for them.

One may ask, "What kind of relationship is marriage?" or "What is marriage?" Marriage is the life-long covenant (contract, or commitment) according to the law of God and the laws of the land, between two eligible persons, of opposite sex (one male and one female) with the privilege of sexual cohabitation. Sexual intercourse with any other partner, before or after the wedding, is adultery. Only within the confines of the home; the husband-wife relationship, may children honorably be born. Marriage is a union that supersedes the parent-child relationship. Marriage is nourished and perpetuated by love, and each spouse is divinely obligated to love his or her marriage partner. The marriage contract should never be terminated, except by the hand of death or adultery (if the innocent partner chooses to end the relationship).

The foundation of the home, as outlined in the above definition, is being undermined by immoral situations and practices. Satan is working to weaken and ultimately destroy our homes and marriages. We must stay alert and be on guard to protect our precious relationships and the pattern of marriage as designed by our Creator.

DURATION

God "hates divorce" (Malachi 2:16). Jesus referred back to the beginning to remind man that God's will is for one man and one woman to be married for the duration of their lifetime (Matthew 19:3-12).

---

2. http://www.albertmohler.com/2010/11/29/who-needs-marriage-time-asked-th-question-do-you-have-an-answer/.

IMPLICATIONS

There is an immediate need for us to work toward making our marriages what God intended them to be. There is a need for the young to be taught what the Bible says about marriage and the family, which will enable future generations to avoid the failures that can occur when the Biblical framework for the family is ignored. The need for the Lord's people to demonstrate and model that marriage can work as God intended, is sorely needed in our society.

What can we learn about the marriage relationship between a man and a woman?

Covenant: Marriage is a covenant existing between a man and a woman. This covenant also includes God (Malachi 2:14-16):

> Yet you say, "For what reason?" Because the LORD has been witness between you and the wife of your youth, with whom you have dealt treacherously; yet she is your companion and your wife by covenant. But did He not make them one, having a remnant of the Spirit? And why one? He seeks godly offspring. Therefore take heed to your spirit, and let none deal treacherously with the wife of his youth. For the LORD God of Israel says That He hates divorce, "For it covers one's garment with violence," Says the LORD of hosts. "Therefore take heed to your spirit, that you do not deal treacherously."[3]

As individuals, we share the marriage with our spouse and our God. The Bible has described our relationship as husband and wife in comparison with the relationship between Christ and His church (Ephesians 5:22-33).

The fundamental biblical description of marriage is

---

3. David Atkinison, *To Have and To Hold* (Grand Rapids: Eerdmans, 1981), 71.

given in covenant terms, and the interchange of analogies by which human marriage is used to describe God's covenant relationship with his people, and by which God's relationship with his people, or Christ's with his church, is used to provide a pattern for human marriage, can be traced through both the Old and New Testaments.[4]

This trio relationship of God, man, and woman is also illustrated in Matthew 19:4-8.

> And He answered and said to them, "Have you not read that He who made them at the beginning 'made them male and female,' and said, 'For this reason a man shall leave his father and mother and be joined to his wife, and the two shall become one flesh'? So then, they are no longer two but one flesh. Therefore what God has joined together, let not man separate. They said to Him, "Why then did Moses command to give a certificate of divorce, and to put her away?" He said to them, "Moses, because of the hardness of your hearts, permitted you to divorce your wives, but from the beginning it was not so.

Jesus sealed the covenant of the marriage bond between man, woman, and God, allowing only sexual infidelity or death to sever it (Matthew 19:9; Romans 7:1-3).

Becoming one implies the intimate association that was planned by God to be between husband and wife.

> The Genesis account shows us that marriage, as designed by God, is a covenant of companionship in which two people become linked in body, soul, and mind. They become, as Genesis 2:24 says, "one flesh."

---

4. Fred Lowery, *Covenant Marriage* (West Monroe, LA: Howard, 2002), 66.

They complete each other and give themselves to each other in a companionship that fills the void in their lives and provides for ultimate happiness and fulfillment. It is the ultimate friendship.[5]

Compatibility: "And the LORD God said, 'It is not good that man should be alone; I will make him a helper comparable to him.'" "Therefore a man shall leave his father and mother and be joined to his wife, and they shall become one flesh" (Genesis 2:18, 24).

Being compatible is part of the beauty and contentment that exists when a man and a woman become one. This compatible relationship involves the fulfilling of needs reciprocally by each spouse. Dr. Willard Harley identifies the "needs" of a man and a woman in *His Needs, Her Needs*.

Her Needs

- Affection
- Conversation
- Honesty and openness
- Financial support
- Family commitment

His Needs

- Sexual fulfillment
- Recreational companionship
- Attractive spouse
- Domestic support
- Admiration

Husbands and wives must communicate to each other their own

---

5. Fred Lowery, *Covenant Marriage* (West Monroe: Howard Publishing, 2002), 66.

specific, personal needs and exhibit love in fulfilling those needs in the marriage. Affection is typically the number one need of a wife; the outward display of tender emotion while sexual fulfillment is typically the husband's number one need. These qualities should be evident in heart and action in the husband and wife. The lists provide each spouse with the knowledge of how they can better support one another between Sundays.

It was T. S. Eliot who said, "Remember, marriage is the greatest test in the world…It is much more than a test of sweetness of temper, as people sometimes think; it is a test of the whole character and affects every action."

Commitment: "Wives, submit to your own husbands, as is fitting in the Lord. Husbands, love your wives and do not be bitter toward them" (Colossians 3:18-19). The commitment is to be long term: "What therefore God has joined together, let not man separate" (Matthew 19:6).

Companionship: "And the LORD God said, 'It is not good that man should be alone; I will make him a helper comparable to him'" (Genesis 2:18). Woman was created and provided by God for man not to be alone. "Monogamous heterosexual marriage was always viewed as the divine norm from the outset of creation." Marriage is the most intimate companionship among God's Creation.

CONSEQUENCES

Marriage and the family provide many positive results that can bring a lifetime of satisfaction.

Marriage is to be an expression of the highest motive known to man – LOVE. "Agape (love) has to do with the mind and the will and is not simply an emotion which rises unbidden in our hearts. It is something which we must deliberately determine to do."[6]

If it is God's plan that there be children in the home, propagation comes from the ordained union. "And God blessed them. And

---

6. William Barclay, *New Testament Words* (Philadelphia: Westminster, 1974), 21.

God said to them, "Be fruitful and multiply and fill the earth and subdue it…" (Genesis 1:28). The avoidance of immorality is clearly evident in God's mandate for marriage. The temptation to circumvent marriage and just move in together ignores God's design of the sacred institution. A casual perusal of the Old and New Testaments raise an awareness of the sinfulness of living together outside of the marriage institution. Becoming "one flesh" in the marriage relationship is clear evidence that sexual relationships outside of marriage are sinful. 1 Corinthians 6:16 defines the "becoming one flesh" of Genesis 2:24 as sexual intercourse. In the case of Genesis 2:24, it is between a husband and a wife. However, in the case of 1 Corinthians 6:16 if it is between a person and a prostitute; both are sinful.

> But because of the temptation to sexual immorality, each man should have his own wife and each woman her own husband. The husband should give to his wife her conjugal rights, and likewise the wife to her husband. For the wife does not have authority over her own body, but the husband does. Likewise the husband does not have authority over his own body, but the wife does.
> 1 Corinthians 7:2-4

MARRYING TO GO TO HEAVEN

Growing in faith, worshipping and serving faithfully, repenting when we sin, and teaching others about Jesus are just a few of the processes and life duties we have as Christians. We understand these to be essential components in our lives as we prepare for eternity. A husband and wife, taking one day at a time, can make their home a wonderful place to live between Sundays by keeping God and Jesus at the center of their union.

A major influence on our lives will come from our spouse.. That being the case, we should recognize the importance in choosing someone that will help us get to Heaven.

God designed marriage as a partnership where both parties are to agree regarding their values, spirituality, eternal goals, and a multiplicity of other things. There are some questions to ask when beginning or considering a relationship:

- Does this person put spiritual values first?
- Will he/she help me to go to Heaven?
- Will I grow spiritually as a result of being married to him/her?
- Does he/she have those characteristics that will make them a godly father/mother to our children?
- Is he/she pure in speech, in body, in action and heart?
- Can I thank God for this person?

Tertullian of Carthage, presented the following in the 2nd Century that highlights the deep abiding connection of a man and a woman who are committed to God and Christ in their relationship:

> How beautiful, then, the marriage of two Christians, two who are one in hope, one in desire, one in the way of life they follow, one in the religion they practice. They are as brother and sister, both servants of the same Master. Nothing divides them, either in flesh or in spirit. They are, in very truth, two in one flesh; and where there is but one flesh there is also but one spirit... [He concludes:] Where there are two together, there also (Christ) is present, and where He is, there evil is not present.[7]

---

7. Tertullian (c. 160-220), "To His Wife" in *Treatises on Marriage and Remarriage*, ACW Series , no. 13, trans. William P. LeSaint, S.J. (Westminster, MD: Newman Press, 1951): 35-36.

CHRISTIAN FAMILY

Being raised by Christian parents is at the top of my list of blessings. Along with grandparents on both sides, the influence of New Testament Christianity was prevalent through uncles, aunts, great uncles and great aunts, cousins and other relatives who had "obeyed from the heart that form of doctrine" (Romans 6:17), were washed in the blood of the Lamb, and had their names enrolled in the Lamb's Book of Life (Revelation 21:27). Memories of songs, worship services, Bible class teachers, older Christian saints and other influences presented a solid foundation early in my life. Atmosphere and environment have much to contribute for who we are. I remember many examples of my family sowing Christian seeds in my life.

Those growing up today need positive and godly influences relative to marriage and the home. Are we doing all we can to ensure this happens? Are we thinking and acting in ways that enrich our marriages between Sundays?

Make sure the one you plan to marry is concerned and committed to helping himself/herself and you, go to Heaven. When a Christian marries a non-Christian or one who is a weak Christian, they may very likely be inviting future marital and spiritual problems into the home.

CHALLENGES

How is your home life between Sundays? God views marriage and the home as an essential element of society. Marriage is not merely a social invention, which can be discarded by society for an arrangement it might like better. On June 26, 2015, the United States Supreme Court redefined marriage. This was not an overnight decision but, in reality, the result of a sexual revolution that began in the twentieth century. However, God instituted and defined marriage long before the Supreme Court announced its opinion.

Homes that honor God and His Word contribute untold good through acts of kindness, morality, and godliness to a world filled with rudeness, sin, and wickedness.

We find many areas that can be challenges to our homes: absentee parents, alcoholism, alternative lifestyles, anti-Christian culture, busyness, child molestation, dishonesty, divorce, euthanasia, financial pressures, gambling, hedonism, homelessness, homosexuality, humanism, immaturity, immoral speech, incest, infanticide, in-laws, lack of communication, living together, materialism, media, minimal interaction, mobility of society, pornography, postmodernism, racism, relativism, sexual immorality, substance addictions, suicide, teen pregnancy, traditional values breakdown, transgenderism, unbalanced work, and family environment.

Many of these have been common to every generation and some are more prevalent at certain times. These and many other issues have the potential to compromise, weaken or destroy what we have built with God and our spouse. What can we do?

> We must contend for marriage as God's gift to humanity-a gift central and essential to human flourishing and a gift that is limited to the conjugal union of a man and a woman. We must contend for religious liberty for all, and focus our energies on protecting the rights of Christian citizens and Christian institutions to teach and operate on the basis of Christian conviction. We cannot be silent, and we cannot join the moral revolution that stands in direct opposition to what we believe the Creator has designed, given, and intended for us. We cannot be silent, and we cannot fail to contend for marriage as the union of a man and a woman.[8]

God's plan for a successful marriage requires commitment and the desire to succeed on our part. May we dedicate ourselves to fulfilling our responsibilities as husbands and wives.

---

8. Albert Mohler, *We Cannot Be Silent* (Nashville: Nelson, 2015), 1-2.

Prayer

God our Father, please help each spouse to fulfill their specific role in our marriages. May we incorporate your Word in every aspect of our marriages and homes and seek purity of life. Help us uphold and be faithful to the vows we made to each other, seeking to honor one another, recognizing you as our Father, and remembering our spouse is a child of yours that you are watching over. Help us through each day as we navigate between Sundays. Thank you for the many blessings the design of marriage brings to us when we follow your Word and practice it with our spouse. In Jesus Name, Amen.

QUESTIONS

1. Discuss the origin of marriage (Genesis 2:18, 24).
2. What is God's will for the duration of a marriage between a man and a woman?
3. What are advantages of a Christian marrying a Christian? What are some disadvantages of a Christian marrying a non-Christian?
4. Why is it important to know the needs of our spouse?
5. Discuss some of the current challenges Christians face regarding marriage and the home.

13

I WILL BE A FAITHFUL MEMBER OF THE BODY

The body of Christ has obligations and a lifestyle to be lived out between Sundays. The Lord's church is called out of the world. God has "delivered us from the power of darkness, and hath translated us into the kingdom of his dear Son" (Colossians 1:13). People who have been added to the body of Christ by the Lord (Acts 2:47) are a cleansed people who have been washed by the blood of Christ. Paul observes our former condition in contrast to what is now enjoyed in Christ: "That at that time ye were without Christ, being aliens from the commonwealth of Israel, and strangers from the covenants of promise, having no hope, and without God in the world: But now in Christ Jesus ye who sometimes were far off are made nigh by the blood of Christ" (Ephesians 2:12-13). Once, we were without the salvation that is found in Jesus Christ, but now we are cleansed and purified by the blood of Christ.

IN CHRIST, IN THE CHURCH

Under the heading, "All Christians Members of the Church," the stalwart H. Leo Boles wrote:

> The Lord adds people to the church (Acts 2:47). The Lord adds to his church those who are called by the gospel. That which makes one a Christian makes one a member of the church. The New Testament does not

teach one process of making people Christians and another process of adding them to the church; hence, the church includes all Christians--that is, the church in its general sense. The church in its local sense includes all Christians in that location. These Christians may not be faithful to the Lord; many of them are not; however, that does not change the New Testament use of the term. God has but one way of making people Christians; he has but one way of adding them to the church. Obedience to the gospel makes one a Christian; obedience to the gospel adds one to the church. There is no such thing in New Testament language as a Christian out of the church of "the Lord. One may belong to a denomination and not belong to the church of the Lord; one even may be a member of the church of Christ and belong to some denomination. A Christian should not belong to a denomination; one is in error who belongs to a denomination All Christians should come out of denominations and be only Christians. They should belong only to the church that Christ called "my church."[1]

As we interact with our friends, co-workers, neighbors, and sometimes family, we often encounter misconceptions of what it means to be a New Testament Christian and a member of the church of Christ. Many fail to comprehend there could only be one body of Christ, and we are to lovingly and truthfully relay the Bible's teaching on Christ and His church (1 Peter 3:15; Matthew 16:18).

ENLIGHTENING OUR RELIGIOUS NEIGHBORS

We expect choice in everything. The Coca-Cola Freestyle machine boasts over 100 drink choices. We choose what we like. When it comes to God and religion, people expect to choose what church

---

1. *Gospel Advocate*, 1940, 53.

they attend and practice with choices that make them feel good.

Am I free to respond to God's grace and be immersed for the forgiveness of my sins and recognize that the Lord places me in His kingdom? Yes. May I meet with a religious group that is not the church described in the New Testament and be pleasing to God? There are many who will disagree with the answer to the second question.

While we are free to choose or reject salvation, we are not given a choice as to where salvation lies. If we choose Christ, we choose His church, which God has already created for us. When it comes to entering the church of Christ, who has commanded the terms of entrance? Christ.

While denominational, community, and satellite groups offer a palate of options for what pleases you, the Son of God offers salvation from your sins by being washed in His blood. It is within this "spiritual house" that we benefit from the atonement provided by the blood of Christ. As Everett Ferguson has written: "The tabernacle and then the temple was the place of the sin offerings and where the people received forgiveness (Leviticus 4-5; 16) …the benefits of that atonement are applied in the earthly community described as a temple (Ephesians 2:13-22). The church is the community of the saved, the people who receive, proclaim, and live by the reconciliation effected by Christ."[2]

Jesus knew many would be misled by false concepts and ideologies when He said: "Not everyone who says to me, 'Lord, Lord,' will enter the kingdom of Heaven, but the one who does the will of my Father who is in Heaven. On that day many will say to me, 'Lord, Lord, did we not prophesy in your name, and cast out demons in your name, and do many mighty works in your name?' And then will I declare to them, 'I never knew you; depart from me, you workers of lawlessness'" (Matthew 7:21-23).

---

2. Everett Ferguson, *The Church of Christ: A Biblical Ecclesiology for Today* (Grand Rapids: Eerdmans, 1996), 129.

NOT A DENOMINATION

Between Sundays, we are confronted with questions about who we are in the churches of Christ. We must endeavor to speak kind words of truth and patiently teach those who inquire about our faith and religious practices.

In 1955 F.W. Mattox wrote *The Eternal Kingdom, A History of the Church of Christ*. His summarization of "restoration," found in the chapter "The Unfinished Restoration" is one of the best statements in print on the subject and can help us in answering who we are:

> The church which Christ built is neither denominational nor Protestant. It possesses no denominating creed, name or hierarchy. It was not founded in protest to any existing institution. It is not the product of the "Reformation" or the "Restoration." But it is, and must be, the full-grown plant which has arisen from the "seed of the kingdom" sown in the hearts of men. Its origin is to be found in the gospel of Christ. It is founded on the apostles and prophets with Christ as the chief corner stone. To date its appearance in history earlier or later than the atonement of Christ is futile, for it is His body and He purchased it with His own blood. By its very nature, the body is exclusive: it is one. There could not conceivably be more than one body as there is but one head. In the presence of a divided Christendom one runs the risk of being misunderstood by suggesting that there is but one church. It is not here suggested that there is but one "denomination." The church of Jesus Christ is neither Jewish, Catholic nor Protestant. It is non-denominational in its origin, worship and organization. It is the body of Christ, functioning according to New Testament directions, organized according to New Testament pattern and worshipping according to New Testa-

ment instructions, extensive enough to embrace in its fellowship all who comply with God's requirements and who thus become a part of that body. Moving on through time to its ultimate victory this "stone cut out of the mountain without hands" survives the rise and fall of temporal kingdoms and proves itself to be that which in reality it is — the Eternal Kingdom."[3]

THE CHURCH IS GOSPEL BORN

It is imperative that between Sundays we remember who we are, and that we are in the greatest institution created for the saved. The Gospel of Christ produced the church of Christ. As it is truthfully stated, without the Gospel, there is no church. The seed of the Gospel sown in honest and genuine hearts produces Christians when individuals render obedience to the plan of salvation.

The conclusion of Peter's sermon in Acts 2 is Jesus of Nazareth is Lord and Christ (2:34-36). This instigated a question from the people and an answer from the Apostle Peter as he and the other apostles were gathered there on the first Pentecost after the resurrection of Christ. "Now when they heard this, they were cut to the heart, and said, 'What shall we do?' Then Peter said ... 'Repent, and let every one of you be baptized in the name of Jesus Christ for the remission of sins; and you shall receive the gift of the Holy Spirit" (Acts 2:37-38). The ones who responded to Peter's inspired sermon are described: "Praising God and having favor with all the people. And the Lord added to their number day by day those who were being saved" (Acts 2:47). This tells us those who respond in obedience (repenting and being immersed in water) receive remission of sins, the gift of the Holy Spirit, and membership in the church of Christ.

Three questions are clarified in this teaching. First, who is the Savior of mankind (Acts 4:12)? Second, when is a person saved (Mark 16:16)? Third, where does Christ save (Ephesians 5:23)? Jesus

---

3. F. W. Mattox, *The Eternal Kingdom* (Delight, AR: Gospel Light, 1961), 350-51.

the Savior, saves us in His body, which is His church, when we obey the Gospel of Christ.

THE CHURCH IS CHRIST CONNECTED

We are Christians at all times, and between Sundays we have the opportunity to let Christ shine through our work and service in the church. The church is Christ's and cannot be separated from Him. "And he put all things under his feet and gave him as head over all things to the church, which is his body, the fullness of him who fills all in all" (Ephesians 1:22-23). Jesus is the head of His body, the church, and the church would not exist without His involvement.

Jesus loved us when we did not deserve it: "But God shows his love for us in that while we were still sinners, Christ died for us" (Romans 5:8). This same love is exhibited toward the church Jesus built: "Christ also loved the church and gave himself up for her" (Ephesians 5:25). The love of Jesus covers those in His body, which will ultimately be delivered to God the Father at the last day (1 Corinthians 15:24).

The church has been purchased by Christ through Jesus giving His life on the cross. In Matthew 16:18 Jesus promised: "On this rock I will build my church." "My" points out two qualities: one is possession and the other is personal. The church is the personal possession of Jesus. He owns it: "which he obtained with his own blood" (Acts 20:28). The Lord eternally saves the body of Christ. "Being himself the savior of the body" (Ephesians 5:23).

Being in Christ is being in the church. The Bible is very explicit in this understanding of how one gets into Christ and into the church of Christ. "For in Christ Jesus you are all sons of God, through faith. For as many of you as were baptized into Christ have put on Christ" (Galatians 3:26-27). "For just as the body is one and has many members, and all the members of the body, though many, are one body, so it is with Christ. For in one Spirit we were all baptized into one body—Jews or Greeks, slaves or free—and all were made to drink of one Spirit" (1 Corinthians 12:12-13).

OUR FOCUS BETWEEN SUNDAYS

Where should our focus lie as the church for which Jesus died? In a world of distractions here are just a few thoughts for your consideration. Between Sundays, we should:

Remain focused on giving glory to God. "So, whether you eat or drink, or whatever you do, do all to the glory of God" (1 Corinthians 10:31).

Remain focused on sharing the salvation found in Jesus Christ. "And Jesus came and said to them, "All authority in heaven and on earth has been given to me. Go therefore and make disciples of all nations, baptizing them in the name of the Father and of the Son and of the Holy Spirit, teaching them to observe all that I have commanded you. And behold, I am with you always, to the end of the age" (Matthew 28:18-20).

Remain focused on keeping unity in the body of Christ. "Eager to maintain the unity of the Spirit in the bond of peace" (Ephesians 4:3).

Remain focused on letting the light of Jesus shine through us. "You are the light of the world. A city set on a hill cannot be hidden. Nor do people light a lamp and put it under a basket, but on a stand, and it gives light to all in the house. In the same way, let your light shine before others, so that they may see your good works and give glory to your Father who is in heaven" (Matthew 5:14-16).

Remain focused on accomplishing good as we go through each day. "So then, as we have opportunity, let us do good to everyone, and especially to those who are of the household of faith" (Galatians 6:10).

Remain focused on continuing our education in God's Word. "Do your best to present yourself to God as one approved, a worker who has no need to be ashamed, rightly handling the word of truth" (2 Timothy 2:15).

Remain focused on prayer to the God of Heaven. "Do not be anxious about anything, but in everything by prayer and supplication with thanksgiving let your requests be made known to God" (Philippians 4:6).

Remain focused on Heaven and all things spiritual. "Set your mind on the things above, not on the things that are on earth" (Colossians 3:2).

BE DISTINCTIVE

God has always called on His people to be distinct and set apart for His purposes while journeying through this world.

God spoke about Israel: "For you are a people holy to the LORD your God. The LORD your God has chosen you to be a people for his treasured possession, out of all the peoples who are on the face of the earth" (Deuteronomy 7:6). New Testament Christians are the people of God today: "But you are a chosen race, a royal priesthood, a holy nation, a people for his own possession, that you may proclaim the excellencies of him who called you out of darkness into his marvelous light. Once you were not a people, but now you are God's people; once you had not received mercy, but now you have received mercy" (1 Peter 2:9-10).

Our distinctiveness from the world is important to God. Phil Sanders notes some of the many distinctions in the Bible that highlight our Christian uniqueness:

> Scripture distinguishes the wide from the narrow (Matthew 7:13-14), the wise from the foolish (Matthew 7:24-27), the world's way from the will of God (Romans 12:2), the domain of darkness from the kingdom of the Son (Colossians 1:13-14), and those who belong to the evil one from those who are born of God (1 John 5:18-19). Scripture clearly distinguishes the one way from all others (John 14:6), the one gospel from all others (Galatians 1:6-9), the one body from all others (Ephesians 1:22-23; 4:4), and the one baptism from all others (Ephesians 4:5).[4]

---

4. Phil Sanders, *Spiritual Sword*, Vol 43, No. 2 (Jan 2012), 23-24.

There is a strong pull on the Christian from the world to align our beliefs, practices, and morals to the surrounding culture. Phil Sanders has accurately highlighted the danger among us to compromise our distinctiveness:

> When people blend God's way with current culture and blur the boundaries of truth and error, they challenge God's place in their lives. Very honestly, some Christians are ashamed of what God's word teaches about music, the women's role in the church, baptism as immersion, the one church, and many other matters. They feel they must reinvent Christianity by editing God's word so as to make it appealing to contemporary culture. By doing this, they presume they are wiser and better than God. Blurring distinctions produces the ultimate blasphemy of God. Unwilling to accept God for who he is, the one who blurs distinctions feels he must remake the Lord in his own image. His invented god believes whatever he decides. Blurring God's distinctions fails to give God the reverence and obedience he deserves. To blur distinctions says to God that he is subject to man rather than man being subject to him.[5]

The danger of losing our distinctiveness lies within us. It is not what is outside the church that is a threat as much as what is inside. Our status in God's sight has been predetermined through the Word of God. Between Sundays we cannot afford to give up or compromise our distinctiveness for the praise of the world and those who care little for Bible authority. Our eternal destiny depends upon our being committed to God's way, by being His children and allowing Him to determine what makes us distinct.

"Do all things without grumbling or disputing, that you may be blameless and innocent, children of God without blemish in

---

5. Ibid.

the midst of a crooked and twisted generation, among whom you shine as lights in the world, holding fast to the word of life, so that in the day of Christ I may be proud that I did not run in vain or labor in vain" (Philippians 2:14-16).

In so many cases it must be admitted that the world is strongly influencing the church toward worldliness, while the church seems to possess little strength to influence the culture toward holiness. It is crucial we maintain our identity as God's people leaving the landmarks of distinctive doctrine in place as God gave it to us (Hosea 5:10; Jude 3). When we do that, God will be glorified and the church will be blessed by Him.

The Divine side of the church is perfect. The human side is imperfect. To be in Christ is to be in His church and to be in His church is to be in Christ. This church is described and identified in the Scriptures in precise terminology so that we can be the church Jesus said He would build.

Our goal is to be the church we read about in the New Testament, nothing more, and nothing less. What a comfort to march in the army that will never know defeat. What a joy it is to be a citizen of a kingdom that will never be destroyed. God's kingdom is a victorious kingdom!

God has:

- A special group of people that He calls His own,
- A special group of people described as a kingdom, a flock, a body, a bride, a family, a church.
- A special group of people that exists as the only group of individuals God claims,
- A special group of people for whom God has reserved every spiritual blessing,
- A special group of people that exists apart from the rest of the religions of the world,
- And a special group of people identified by the specifics, the pattern, of Scripture.

Our walk with God between Sundays is not a journey we make alone. God, our Lord Jesus Christ, and the Holy Spirit are with us each day. They provide us direction, encouragement, and edification, while at the same time rebuking us and exposing our sins, yet providing forgiveness when we repent and walk in the light, all the while giving our God the best we have to offer in every area of our lives. May we remember the remarkable opportunities and blessings provided for us by the Godhead every day of the week. "What then shall we say to these things? If God is for us, who can be against us" (Romans 8:31).

QUESTIONS

1. Discuss how salvation is found in Christ and also in His body, which is the church.
2. Explain the concept that the New Testament church is pre-denominational.
3. Using Matthew 16:18, discuss the two points of ownership Christ has over the church.
4. What identifying marks are unique to the churches of Christ, as found in God's Word?
5. Discuss the differences between the divine side and the human side of the church.

ACKNOWLEDGMENTS

Any endeavor (in this case, writing a book) involves influential and encouraging hands. The following have been instrumental in accomplishing this goal.

My parents Charles (1929-2013) and Betty (Hannah) (1932-2009) Miller always encouraged and supported me in preaching, teaching, and writing. They each embodied a strong dedication to the Lord and His Church, as well as a solid Christian work ethic.

My first editor, Betty Ann Miller (1922-2017), a college professor in English, marked up (in red ink) my feeble attempts at writing articles early on and was another encourager in my family.

My wife Deanna has motivated and supported me to follow my dreams and goals. God has truly blessed me with greatness in Deanna. The support of my children brightens each day: thank you Chelsea and Isaiah.

Mark and Alicia McKenzie made possible the publishing of this volume. I am deeply indebted to them for untold kindnesses through the years. Their friendship has been unwavering, and I am thankful for their love and support.

Thank you, Sheila Butt for reading the manuscript and offering valuable insight. You are a highly respected and influential servant and have done much through your writings and work in the kingdom.

I appreciate David R. Pharr for reading the manuscript and giving encouragement for it being published.

Michael Whitworth, thank you for reading my manuscript and

your willingness to publish it. I appreciate your work and your personal dedication to seeing this project through to completion. Your passion for God and His Word is evident in all that you do for Christ and His Church.

Made in United States
North Haven, CT
29 June 2023